"As Christians, we often talk a_____ spiritual growth,' but for many it's a concept that remains elusive. With *Unstuck*, Michael Ross and Arnie Cole offer a blueprint for genuine growth in grace, grounded in the life-changing power of Scripture."

—Jim Daly, President, Focus on the Family

"Arnie Cole and Michael Ross's new book *Unstuck* is a gem. Written in an engaging, transparent way, *Unstuck* offers tremendous insights on growing a close relationship with Christ and living a transformed, fruitful, and vibrant spiritual life—rather than a frustrating, "stuck" one."

—Cheri Fuller, Author of *The Busy Woman's Guide to Prayer; The One-Year Book of Praying Through the Bible*

"Disconnected, spiritually empty, *stuck*. We've all been there. This book gets us moving again through the eternal, transformational Word of God. *Unstuck* is an important resource for churches, families—everyone!"

—H. B. London, Bestselling Author and Pastor to Pastor Emeritus, Focus on the Family

"Fascinating—from the first page to the very last word! This compelling read underscores the importance of God's Word. It's like a cup of life-giving water for a thirsty soul. *Unstuck* is heartfelt, convicting, powerful, and hard to put down."

—Richard P. Bott II, President, Bott Radio Network

Unstuck

Michael Ross

Unstuck

Your Life. God's Design. Real Change.

Arnie Cole + Michael Ross

BETHANY HOUSE PUBLISHERS
a division of Baker Publishing Group
Minneapolis, Minnesota

© 2012 by Arnie Cole and Michael Ross

Published by Bethany House Publishers
11400 Hampshire Avenue South
Bloomington, Minnesota 55438
www.bethanyhouse.com

Bethany House Publishers is a division of
Baker Publishing Group, Grand Rapids, Michigan

Printed in the United States of America

Library of Congress Cataloging-in-Publication Data

Cole, Arnie
    Unstuck : your life, God's design, real change / Arnie Cole and Michael Ross.
      p.   cm.
    Summary: "Using information from extensive survey research, the authors give readers a practical and proven way to daily engage with Scripture, connect with God, and increase their faith"—Proved by publisher.
    Includes bibliographical references.
    ISBN 978-0-7642-0954-3 (pbk. : alk. paper)
    1. Spiritual formation. 2. Spiritual life—Christianity. 3. Christian life.
I. Ross, Michael. II. Title
BV4511.C548 2012
248.4—dc23   2012001915

All events/accounts in this book are factual. Some names and small details have been changed in order to protect the privacy of those involved.

The internet addresses, email addresses, and phone numbers in this book are accurate at the time of publication. They are provided as a resource. Baker Publishing Group does not endorse them or vouch for their content or permanence.

In keeping with biblical principles of creation stewardship, Baker Publishing Group advocates the responsible use of our natural resources. As a member of the Green Press Initiative, our company uses recycled paper when possible. The text paper of this book is composed in part of post-consumer waste.

Cover design by Lookout Design, Inc.

Authors are represented by WordServe Literary Group

12   13   14   15   16   17   18   7   6   5   4   3   2   1

75173357

From Arnie

To all the special people who have traveled with me on my spiritual journey . . .

my mom and dad, Dr. Ken and Ruth Cole, who prayed for me more than twenty-five years while I was spiritually stuck

my brothers and sisters, Wes and Lou Ann, and Kathy and Dean, for hanging in through all the drama

my pastor, Gary Inrig, who helped me find "True North"

my friend and mentor Dr. Woodrow Kroll, who asked, "Why do so many Christians own Bibles and never read them?"

my friend Bill Bantz, who demanded we help people positively engage their spiritual life on a daily basis

my researchers Pam and LG, who made sure we got it right

my kids, Ben, Matt, Danny, and Laura, who love me despite my shortcomings

my wife and love of my life, Char, who knew all my past failures, who believed in me before I did, and who gave me a chance

my Lord Jesus Christ, who saved me from spiritual death

From Michael

To my brothers, Robert, Jerry, and Walter

"Christ says, 'Give me All. . . . I want you. I have not come to torment your natural self, but to kill it. No half-measures are any good. I don't want to cut off a branch here and a branch there. I want to have the whole tree down. Hand over the whole natural self, all the desires which you think innocent as well as the ones you think wicked—the whole outfit. I will give you a new self instead. In fact, I will give you Myself: my own will shall become yours.'"[1]

Contents

Acknowledgments

Come meet the amazing team that helped us make this book a reality. These folks are much more than media and ministry professionals; they are our friends.

Dr. Woodrow Kroll—president of Back to the Bible. His guidance and skill as a Bible expert and teacher has been a tremendous help to us.

Dr. Pamela Ovwigho—executive director of the Center for Bible Engagement. She directed all the research that became this book's foundation.

Theresa Cox—writer, missionary, and a physician's assistant in Colorado. She contributed her story in chapters 6 and 10.

Tiffany Ross—wife, mother, and children's director in Nebraska. She contributed theological insights and also her story in chapter 11.

Char Cole—wife, mother, and co-owner of Still Waters Ranch in Nebraska. She offered invaluable editorial suggestions.

Margie Younce—program director for a nonprofit social outreach in West Virginia. She contributed to the chapter 5 story "Getting Unstuck Means Digging Deep."

Manfred Koehler—writer, missionary, and a businessman in Ontario. He provided biblical research and contributed to portions of chapter 13.

David Barshinger—writer, and PhD candidate at Trinity Evangelical Divinity School. He contributed to portions of chapter 5, specifically about the life of Paul.

Dr. Mary Spaulding—biblical studies and Hebrew instructor in Colorado Springs and Nairobi, Kenya. She provided insights in chapter 8 on better understanding the Bible.

Greg Johnson—president of WordServe Literary Group in Colorado. He represented *Unstuck* and walked us through the amazing process of creating a book . . . from start to finish.

Kyle Duncan—who acquired this project for Bethany House.

The Minnesota-based editorial and marketing teams at Bethany House—Christopher Soderstrom, Julie Smith, Andy McGuire, Brett Benson, Jim Hart, Carra Carr, Tim Peterson, Steve Oates, David Horton, and Jim Parrish.

Take a bow, friends . . . take a bow!

Starting Point

When Faith Gets Stuck

"I have come that they may have life, and have it to the full."

—John 10:10

Something's gone wrong.

Praying doesn't seem to work anymore; I'm bored with church, and the church crowd. Half the time the Bible doesn't make sense to me—that is, when I slow down enough to actually read it (which isn't often). If I'm really honest with myself, I don't have a clue what God is like . . . or what He wants from me.

I play church and act as if I have it all together. But inside, I'm tired.

Tired of the fog, tired of running hard but never getting anywhere, tired of faking it, tired of missing the things I want most: real purpose . . . real life.

My faith isn't working—and I don't know how to fix it.

Maybe you've been having similar thoughts. It's like a three-hundred-pound gorilla is sharing the room with you. You can see it, others probably can't—yet you're terrified to open your mouth. *What would they think?*

We're talking about the disconnected sense you wake up with most Sundays; an annoying thought that grows into a big hairy beast when worship hour rolls around. It starts beating its chest whenever the congregation breaks into songs like "Amazing Grace."

Yes, I'm a wretch. Yes, I've been saved. Yet most days I'm still *pretty lost, and horribly blind. My life is supposed to be different—somehow* better *than it is now. But it isn't. Something's gone wrong.*

The thing is, the gorilla doesn't just come around Sunday mornings. It sometimes hangs around 24/7. You've tried to live with it, even ignore it. Nothing's worked.

Like we said, you're not the only one struggling spiritually. In this book you'll . . .

Meet Theresa. She was raised in a legalistic church and told that staying in line, following the rules, steering clear of life's "don'ts" would make her acceptable to God. "Read your Bible, go to church, and say your prayers," was her preacher's motto. One night Theresa, who was twenty-four at the time, woke up in a cold sweat: *Is this really it? Just rules and checklists and striving to get stamped with approval? Something's gone wrong.*

Meet Gene. He'd battled a porn addiction that began at age twelve. Each Sunday this church leader was all smiles and handshakes. The rest of the week this middle-aged man lost most days spiritually before they began. *I know old struggles don't always go away when you give your life to Jesus. I don't know any man who's never fallen to temptation. Yet I've been a believer most of my life. Something's gone wrong.*

14

Meet Kelly. Her family had money and prestige: a palatial home in the nicest part of town, expensive cars, designer clothes, popular friends—everything girls her age think they want. If only they knew her parents abused alcohol—and her. Belt buckles. Dark closets. Nightmares. Unthinkable dysfunction. Eventually Kelly grew up, moved out . . . and tried to convince herself that the past was finally behind her. And she hoped it was. *But I can't seem to trust anyone—not my pastor, not my husband, not even God. I'm thirty-eight, and anxious and angry all the time. I want to let go and move on, but I can't. Something's gone wrong.*

Meet Shane. He was quick to admit his life was a mess— started out that way. His parents abandoned him when he was small, pawning him off on his grandmother. Things got messier through the years, mostly because of alcohol and drug abuse. He hit rock bottom at twenty-four when he spent time behind bars. Then he met Jesus. Now the thirty-four-year-old lives happily ever after . . . right? Not exactly. *I thought I'd get better at relationships, but my own marriage ended in divorce. How could I fall back into old habits? I was supposed to be different, yet I'm moving backward. Something's gone wrong.*

Meet Tiffany. She has what so many other women desire: a loving husband, a healthy son, a fulfilling career. So why can't she sleep at night? Why does the weight of the world seem to press in on her, day after day? *I committed my heart to Jesus at age five. I practically grew up in church—I work in one today. I serve as director of children's ministries—a job I love. So why do I battle anxiety? Why am I so full of fear? Something's gone wrong.*

Meet Arnie. For many years he was a self-described hippie, beach bum, surfer, partier, social activist, cruiser. He plunged headfirst into anything that seemed to make him happy. Add excessive drug and alcohol abuse in his earlier years, an egocentric heart, a cocky swagger . . . it was a lethal mix. Yet by the world's standards, he was a success. Doctor Arnie had carved out a comfortable life. He rubbed elbows with an academic crowd and did groundbreaking work. So why was he miserable? *As a boy, my parents taught me to respect God, but I've grown into a "spiritual loser." My life feels meaningless. Something's gone wrong.*

Meet Mike. He headed up a popular magazine for a large ministry and got to wear many hats: journalist, author, speaker, creative team leader, radio show "expert." Yet he lived in a safe Christian bubble—cut off from the real problems of the real world. Little by little, he became distracted, bored . . . actually disconnected from the God he claimed to serve. Mike's work began to swallow up his identity. *What happened to the real person inside? What happened to the man I used to be: child of God, servant of the Most High, Christ-follower? Something's gone wrong.*

Does your story sound like one or more of these? Maybe you likewise feel as if the Christian life just isn't working. Maybe you've also felt that something's gone desperately wrong.

But what if our lives could be better?

What if we could get unstuck from the things holding us down?

What if our faith could be fresh again?

What if what we need most is right in front of us?

Current research into the spiritual lives of seventy thousand Americans—of all ages, from nearly every corner of the nation—is proving something many Christians have doubted: There's power in God's Word. A majority of those we surveyed showed us that consistently engaging the Bible is *the* key to knowing God intimately, getting unstuck, and growing spiritually.

Yes, it really works—despite what we may have been told! The sixty-six love letters from our Creator are far from irrelevant. To the contrary, getting God's words from our head to our heart (and eventually into our feet) can result in amazing changes that transform how we think, love, live, and serve.

Just ask people like Theresa, Tiffany, Arnie, and Mike.

What have they learned about the Bible that you need to know?

How is it that a book they once viewed as a chore to read is now vital, transformational, *the* answer to their thriving lives? You'll hear and hopefully be inspired by their stories and others. (We're Arnie and Mike—you just met us above and we'll share more below.)

What you won't find are fatigued formulas and familiar guarantees that never pan out. The research we share is quantified and proven, not opinion. You'll get guidance for getting unstuck. You'll discover why it's important to begin thinking biblically, living relationally, and following Christ radically.

We'll Face the Problems

In Part One, we'll explore what goes wrong for most of us: everything from burnout and busyness to our attempts at squeezing new life out of dead things. We'll zero in on the Bible and why it's the bestseller many won't read. *What exactly is this timeless book, and how can it change our lives? If it is life-changing, why aren't we tapping in to it?* We'll round out this section with research eye-openers: A sub-study of more than eight thousand mature believers has given a startling picture of temptation's effects in our lives. Folks in this group confessed that they're beaten down by sin and confused about what true spiritual growth really looks like—or how to experience it.

We'll Look at What Works

In Part Two, we'll dig deep into a relational way of experiencing God's Word. It's about not just reading but engaging the Bible—receiving Scripture with our minds and our hearts, reflecting on God's story, and responding to His message in a personal way. *Doing this consistently is transformational!* It helps us navigate spiritual fog, withstand temptation, and discover the answers God wants to share with us. We describe this process as getting "Powered by Four": (1) Spending time with God (2) Getting refreshed through His Word (3) Being recharged through the Bible (4) Having a meaningful two-way connection with Him. (This will make sense later.) The goal is *relationship*. As we allow more of Jesus Christ in our lives—more of His heart, more of His story, more of what He wants for each of us—the more we learn and grow. And as truth is worked into our own hearts, we learn how to . . .

> . . . *develop the right mindset so we can better live the words of Jesus*
> . . . *take our eyes off ourselves and begin to love others*
> . . . *pray with power and passion*
> . . . *nurture our families*
> . . . *live well and healthy within the community of believers*
> . . . *serve the needy*
> . . . *praise and worship our Creator*
> . . . *become more like Jesus*
> . . . *get unstuck spiritually*

We'll Chart a Plan That Works for You

In Part Three, you'll see how to apply principles of Bible engagement to your own experience. We have within our grasp a key that unlocks spiritual awakening—the answer to a thriving faith! By truly engaging the Scriptures, we can explore timeless truths, discover hope, tap into wisdom, and find our life's purpose. We'll develop an accurate view of God, learn how to "put on" the Bible's protective armor and overcome temptation—and we'll figure out how to get unstuck, again and again.

So, What Are We Getting Into Together?

Is this an anti-formula manual for spiritual growth?
Is it a detailed look at groundbreaking research?
Is it a devotion guide for individual or group studies?

It's all three. *Unstuck* is about spiritual growth and getting the life that matters most. Study these pages on your own, often referring back to them as you would with any practical reference guide. Better yet, read it with friends in whatever small group fits you best.

At the end of each chapter, you'll find three helpful features:

Research Reveals—a significant finding from our analysis. For left-brainers, our conclusions about why Christians stall and what helps them grow are drawn from years of research (conducted by Arnie and the Center for Bible Engagement, a division of Back to the Bible). A team of smart folks is studying the spiritual lives of thousands of Christians, ranging in age from eight to eighty. What we say in these pages is tested and trustworthy.

Encouraging Nudge—a thought-provoking nugget from our conversation. There are several principles we don't want you to miss as we navigate the process of getting spiritually unstuck. We've highlighted those nuggets in these sections, along with action points you can apply to your life.

Spiritual Stepping Stones—a suggested forty-five-day journey through the Bible. It's impossible to convey biblical truths without learning what God's Word says. That's why this book's core spiritual growth principles come straight from Scripture. We want this resource to be much more than another resource *about* the Bible. *Unstuck* will move you deeper into it, challenging you to consume and engage, reflect on and live out God's Word. Along with verses you can study, you'll find questions to help you ponder what you've read. Tackle them on your own or with a study group.

goTandem—a website that will help you and your church grow. In a few spots we invite you to pop over to www.unstuck. gotandem.com for clips to watch, for growth assessments, and for additional faith-building resources.

Give it a try for a taste of what you can experience in the days ahead.

Note: because the personal pronoun *I* can get a little confusing, to keep things simple we'll let you know who's talking when we use it. (For example, in chapter 1, it's Arnie. In chapter 2, it's Mike.) The collective *we* always refers to you and us . . . humans with flaws, wounds, and struggles who want to live a little more like Jesus every day.

Part One
Why We Stall Out

By the End of Part One You'll Be Able to:

- Identify the issues that most often cause Christ-followers to stall
- Recognize the destructive forces seeking to harm every believer
- Know your own hot-button spots (what keeps you from growing)
- Understand why the Bible is essential to spiritual growth
- See how to get moving toward maturity

one

Confessions of a Spiritual Loser

The pessimist complains about the wind; the optimist expects it to change; the realist adjusts the sails.[1]

—William Arthur Ward

Bad habits, addictions, a trail of broken relationships, waking up dead inside—I don't know how many times during my decades away from faith I (Arnie) had told myself, "You are just one big mess. A big-time loser when it comes to any kind of relationship."

At least once a day.

Do you, personally, relate to this? Do you ever regret the way important parts of your own life have turned out? Ever feel stuck in the muck of your lousy choices? Worse, do you think you're going nowhere spiritually . . . does your very soul seem numb?

I felt that way for more than half my life. Yet to my surprise, in some great ways I've broken through. While I certainly don't have a perfect walk of faith, I keep experiencing many more good days than bad. That's why I'm so passionate about what you're going to read.

Maybe you go to church (or have in the past), take part in a Bible study, volunteer occasionally, and do your best to live right. At day's end, though, much of the time, do you feel you're "in a dry and parched land where there is no water"?[2] Perhaps no matter how hard you try, nothing seems to move you closer to God. Could be that the more things you attempt to do that seem "Christian," the less alive you feel.

That's exactly how it was for me, anyway. For years and years I was spiritually *stuck*. Growing up, I was immersed in wise thoughts and advice about life from some wonderful people: my parents, a few well-meaning folks at church, coaches, teachers. It was, at the time, just what every child needed.

But as I hit my late teens and early twenties, I started seeing chinks in the armor of leaders—moral failures, hypocrisy. And then my own behavior started to go south as well. The more difficult my life became, the more I prayed, asking God to save me from whatever problem I had gotten myself into. Yet the more I called out, the farther away God seemed to be. And He never answered my shouts for rescue—or so it seemed to me.

Diving into humanistic psychology, I was exposed to a whole universe of ideas and actions that didn't always match up with Jesus' take on life. I was told that "god" is in every one of us, and that if we're smart enough to break away from our messed-up "religious hang-ups" we can be as free as birds. Slowly but surely I was being hand-sold anti-biblical thoughts, with the corresponding anti-biblical actions following pretty closely behind—all in the name of having "a free spirit." Sadly, twenty-seven years later, I was so confused

I couldn't recognize spiritual truth. I ended up calling bad "good" and good "bad." My theme song was Peggy Lee's "Is That All There Is?"

While it seemed fun at the time, I was a miserable spiritual loser.

In my "freedom from religion," thinking I controlled my destiny, I occasionally got the impression that maybe everything wasn't so great about this "enlightened liberty." When I was thirty, for example, I completed my massive dream house but still wasn't happy or fulfilled. Somehow I became obsessed with the notion of hanging myself from a balcony off the courtyard. Something was terribly wrong in the world I'd created for myself.

However, about fifteen years ago I launched into the process of getting unstuck . . . a process that for me happened very slowly. As I looked back at my old life, I began to see the irony of it all: My quest to be free and to become my own god was, in reality, turning me into a slave. I was in bondage to selfishness, pride, lust, depravity, and—though then I wouldn't have labeled it this way—my own twisted sin nature.

Soon I faced a new challenge: *How do I become free spiritually?*

The more I thought about my failed relationships, the more constantly overwhelmed I became. *LOSER—that's all I've ever been and ever will be.*

One truth gradually and eventually came to change everything. I realized that *I have to win today if I'm going to win the race in all of my tomorrows.*

While it sounded a bit cliché, it made sense. *I have to win* today. *That's all I need to focus on!* While I couldn't change yesterday (or just about anything in my past), it didn't have to define who I am and what I do *today.*

It's as simple and as hard as that.

Simple.

Hard.

Spiritual losers can get unstuck and become winners as they focus on today and connect with Jesus consistently and genuinely. Too often, even devoted Christ-followers forget we have a personal, relatable, and persistent Savior who loves us fully despite our sin and flaws.

Jesus forgets our yesterdays and reminds us not to worry about our tomorrows. Yesterday is there to be learned from, not stuck in. And the worries of tomorrow must be released to God. We can't tightly clutch tomorrow no matter how hard we try to grasp it—God owns tomorrow.

I've learned these truths the hard way. (Later I'll share more.) Dealing well with yesterday and tomorrow is crucial in getting unstuck spiritually.

From Misery to Mastery

In order to convey what a dramatic shift it was for me to trust God with my life again, let me share a bit more of my history by hitting *rewind*. . . .

Despite growing up in a Christian home, from ages twenty to forty-seven I cared more about money and pleasure than people. (Obviously, I'd left God back in Sunday school.) For nearly three decades I was spiritually lost *and* somewhat of a success by our culture's standards.

I'd achieved my doctorate and worked with people who had developmental disabilities. Through carefully developed systems, I helped them change their behaviors so they could one day leave the state-run institutions they'd been forced to call home. (Many were violent and seriously brain damaged.) Two mottos defined my work: "We can't *make* you better; we can only help you to *do* better" and "Work for pay the

American way." To my satisfaction, the majority improved and made their way back into society. The programs I helped develop throughout California were highly in demand.

Financially, life was comfortable, and in my mid-thirties, boating became a passion. When I wasn't working, I was on the Pacific waters; this had become my greatest spiritual high and the place I felt closest to nature. It's where I imagined God liked to hang out.

A world-renowned surfer once said, "Never turn your back on the ocean." Many looked up to the Hawaiian Duke Kahanamoku even more as a spiritual teacher than as an athlete. He believed "contemplation of the waters of creation stimulates extreme emotion—a warm sunset over the island of Oahu inspires peace; a massive storm surge pounding the island's north shore demands fear and respect."[3] As a non-believer, I lived those words. But fear of the thundering seas brought me back to my senses . . . and to my God.

It was 1997. I'd just turned forty-seven, when my wife and I had to face the unthinkable: I was diagnosed with Alzheimer's disease. If I was lucky, I had three good years left.

We sold our businesses, bought a bigger cruising powerboat (we named her *Kindred Spirit*), and decided we'd just sail away. Char and I were at peace on, and continually awed by, the ocean. Like an old friend, the ocean was always familiar, yet always changing too. At least temporarily, we didn't have to focus on the ugly reality staring us in the face.

Later that year I plotted a course from our home in Newport Beach to Alaska, imagining it as my last great adventure before I left this world. Char and I agreed I should take this trip alone—actually, with two male buddies. We'd take turns maneuvering the craft, giving me plenty of time to think and to reflect.

We were headed for some of the world's most dangerous and spectacular cruising grounds. Along Alaska's rug-
ged shores, the scenery from our fifty-five-footer was jaw-
dropping: jagged, snowcapped mountains descended into
the Pacific, ancient spruce forests lined misty beaches, and
eagles—literally dozens—shrieked and circled above us. We
sailed by a glacier and watched as chunks of ice the size of
houses tumbled into the bluest water we'd ever seen. One
morning we were close enough to a humpback whale to hear
it blow and slap the waves with its giant tail.

I remember thinking, *This sure beats sitting in a nursing
home!*

But tranquility soon turned to terror.

On day seven we were around two hundred miles from the
Straits of Juan de Fuca. Our routing service said we could
avoid an oncoming storm if we made our way to the safety
of the Inside Passage. However, instead of heading out when
we were told, we cut the engine and decided to party. That
nine-hour mistake nearly cost us our lives.

We heard a growl a long way off, toward the heart of the
storm. It built like a crescendo, growing louder and louder.
Suddenly, violent waves rolled down upon us as if we'd been
tossed into a rampage.

We're not going to survive this, I thought. *Our time is up.*

I called Char and tried desperately to hide my panic. Tears
rolled down my face as I told her I loved her with all my
heart. I told her not to worry, even as I knew it was too late.

My heart beat wildly, pumping adrenaline throughout my
body. My pulse raced and my hands trembled as I fought to
head the boat into the massive seas and maintain control.
Each mammoth wave felt like a hundred fire hoses exploding
across the bow.

I kept my cool and, bizarrely, I nearly started to enjoy the fight of my life . . . until we got radio news that two nearby ships had experienced rogue waves—water walls twice as high as we'd already encountered; waves moving in multiple directions. I knew we were toast.

I tried using positive-thinking techniques to help keep composure, but in those moments I didn't have any more ultimate control then any of us ever actually have. At that horrifying time, all I could do was cry out to Jesus, trust that He hadn't given up on me, and then hold on for dear life.

You can guess what happened next. Obviously, we survived, and somehow with only a few minor bruises. The storm died down, and we steered away. The next morning, at the wheel, I prayed for the first time in ages.

Though I don't mind the term *Christian,* admittedly it has a lot of baggage attached to it. Instead of praying to "become a Christian," I told God I wanted to lay aside my old way of life and learn what it meant to live by His ways. I'd always admired what I'd read and heard about the life of Christ, so I called myself a Christ-follower, because this allowed me not to compare the new life I wanted with the old life I'd lived.

Char supported me every step of the way, and in the following months our whole world began to change radically. We began going to church, and we started asking, "Lord, what are you going to do with our lives now?" We earnestly sought to go wherever He might lead in the months I had left.

Little did I realize He was leading me *BACK TO THE BIBLE!* (first to the actual book, and then to the ministry that would result).

While my heart was changing, the wounds from my past didn't heal instantly. If allowed, these injuries can defeat us before we even get started. In addition, the shame of the damage we've done to self and to others can haunt us and, if permitted, undercut our best-laid plans to live as a new person.

Whenever my pastor would talk about certain things, I would cringe. *If people knew the real me, they'd kick me out of this place.* When my group would delve into "living a life that honors Jesus," waves of shame would wash over me, and I'd wonder how I could ever serve God.

Here's what I finally learned: Jesus has relentless tenderness and compassion for us *just as we are*—and not despite our sins and faults but in them and through them. Brennan Manning—a fellow spiritual-loser-turned-Christ-follower—explains it this way: "God won't stop working on us until the job is complete, and God doesn't hold back His love [just] because there is evil in us. Not now, not ever."[4]

Oh yeah . . . and my diagnosis of Alzheimer's, and the short time I was given to live? I didn't die! (Clearly, right?) All symptoms that had led up to the diagnosis had completely disappeared.

I'd been thoroughly examined by renowned medical specialists. I'm absolutely convinced this was a miracle. God still has an important assignment for me in this world.

He has one for you too. *Let's get unstuck!*

Commitment: We Give Up Formula Faith . . . and Experience a Real Relationship With God

Even though my parents did everything in their power to give me the right start in life, I still ended up miserable and disconnected from God. From high school through young adulthood I tried to follow formulas—you know, living by the "eight easy elements" or the "two true tenets" or the "four spiritual laws." I thought good performance guaranteed success. Was I ever *wrong!*

When all the canned processes and remedies with acronyms didn't make a difference, and when Jesus didn't see my efforts and just set everything right . . . and when my life flew out of control and God didn't stop me . . . well, that's when I figured this stuff was all some sort of cruel joke. I angrily threw out the whole idea.

I know now: *If faith is based on formulas, we've taken God out of the formula.*

My middle years have involved a drawn-out path to becoming spiritually unstuck, and I've come to realize this doesn't happen overnight. During my own quest, I've observed way too many believers basing their faith on the latest self-help source instead of the Source of truth. Following the crowd instead of the Creator will always leave us empty—even dead inside.

In one sense, there are two types of Christians:

Notional Christ-followers believe in their concept of Christ; interaction is one-way only.

Relational Christ-followers have a two-way relationship with the true Christ of the Bible.

Disconnecting ourselves from Jesus, ignoring God's Word, and getting caught up in the subculture's perks and quirks or "club Christianity" is downright dangerous. We end up clueless about basic truths, vulnerable to false teaching, spiritually immature, and reflecting on a fantasy-based image of our Creator.

To be brutally honest, lasting growth simply doesn't happen through books about the Bible or in "six simple steps," despite popular promises. *And that's good news.* Finally we can get past the guilt of not living up to other people's expectations. We can be free to live as God's child, free to mature and grow exactly as He intends for each of us individually.

Relationship makes all the difference. Specifically, relationship with the God of the Bible—not my notion, not your notion of God, but *the real God*: the one who loves unconditionally, who's able to heal the soul radically, who forgives completely . . . and who's made a way to move us from death to life.

Commitment: We Stop Casually Reading the Bible . . . and Start Engaging It

The Holy Scriptures. Just hearing those words, some people instantly think of pulpit-pounding preachers or uptight ladies in bright floral dresses. They think of ninety-pound coffee table Bibles more for decoration than transformation. For me, it once brought to mind a scroll-full of rigid rules that seemed largely if not completely beyond my real-world-context ability to follow.

If you think this way, you're not alone.

Almost half the North American Christians I've surveyed don't read or engage the Bible daily. And that same number didn't know what it is or what it's for.

Pretty scary, as the Bible is the key to changing our hearts.

More guaranteed good news, though: Consistent connection with God's Word changes the things about us we want left in the trash can. It helps us handle struggles, resist temptation, live more peacefully and harmoniously.

There's nothing like the written Word of God for showing you the way to salvation through faith in Christ Jesus. Every part of Scripture is God-breathed and useful one way or another—showing us truth, exposing our rebellion, correcting our mistakes, training us to live God's way. Through the Word we are put together and shaped up for the tasks God has for us.[5]

32

Supernatural, transformational, life-changing . . . there's no similar resource. Think about how it came to us! Norman Geisler notes that this alone is amazing:

> First, there is the source of inspiration: God; second, the means of inspiration: men of God; third, the nature of inspiration: words from God: and finally, the result of this inspiration: the divine truth of God. No other book has been composed in this fashion.[6]

Commitment: We Eat Up God's Word Regularly . . . and Tap Into a Two-Way Conversation

To grow in grace, we need more than casual reads of Scripture. We need to feed on what God says to us. We need to digest it. Here's how Eugene Peterson explains Bible engagement:

> Reading is an immense gift, but only if the words are assimilated, taken into the soul—eaten, chewed, gnawed, received in unhurried delight. Words of men and women long dead, or separated by miles and/or years, come off the page and enter our lives freshly and precisely, conveying truth and beauty and goodness, words that God's Spirit has used and uses to breathe life into our souls.[7]

———————

Giving up religion.

Stopping the casual reads, beginning to engage God's Word instead.

Ceasing to fly through "have-to quiet times," developing a meaningful, life-altering, two-way communication with the Lord who loves us.

It is as simple and as hard as this.

I'm not going to kid you: What your heart tells you to *do* won't be easy. Lasting spiritual growth involves movement. Maybe it will mean crawling out of a pit and shaking off shame. Almost certainly it'll involve turning away from and rejecting lies you've swallowed about faith, God, and growth. It'll mean walking day by day on a path whose very ground is alive.

And at times you'll need to run. The Holy Spirit will nudge you, and it will be up to you to sprint fast and far from entanglements and into the arms of Jesus. *That* will mean admitting your flaws, frailties, frustrations . . . and you'll be safe to do this in a relationship of unconditional love and trust.

If *easy* is what you want, go ahead and trade this book for the remote.

But if you're sick of being weighed down and tripped up by the same mistakes, if you're done being paralyzed by legalism, if you can no longer stand choking on religion instead of thriving on relationship . . . if you want forward positive movement and want to truly *live* again, please, keep reading.

In chapter 2, Mike talks openly about wandering in his own spiritual desert, then looks at reasons Christians give for neglecting their faith and ignoring God's Word.

Research Reveals: It's no secret: Life, faith, and spiritual growth are often messy and unpredictable. The truth is, we don't mature and move toward God in a sequential and linear fashion. Spiritual growth moves in multiple directions (toward self and toward Christ) all at once. Accepting this is important for getting unstuck.

Encouraging **Nudge:** "Do not conform to the pattern of this world, but be transformed by the renewing of your mind."[8] God's primary means of bringing about this mind renewal—as well as disarming and destroying spiritual threats and footholds—is His Word. Only truth undoes untruth.

Take a look at unstuck.gotandem.com for more practical ways to grow spiritually. Do this every day during your forty-five-day journey.

Spiritual
Stepping Stones

● **DAY 1**

Scripture to Remember: Revelation 21:1–4

Question to Consider: What causes me to feel hopeless at times?

● **DAY 2**

Scripture to Remember: 1 Peter 2:19–25

Question to Consider: If running toward God is how to grow spiritually—especially when I face seemingly insurmountable challenges—what tends to hold me back from doing this?

● **DAY 3**

Scripture to Remember: 2 Timothy 3:10–17

Question to Consider: In my heart of hearts, do I trust God's Word? Do I trust its Author? (Why, or why not?)

two

"A Thousand Steps" Between Us and God

God will whisper. He will shout. He will touch and tug. He will take away our burdens; He'll even take away our blessings. If there are a thousand steps between us and Him, He will take all but one. But He will leave the final one for us. The choice is ours.[1]

—Max Lucado

A few years back I (Mike) found myself in a spiritual desert. I'd been a Christ-follower more than twenty-six years—experiencing God's presence on most days, sensing His love and direction, feeling connected to Him—and then . . . nothing.

I was in a fog.

Off and on for about six months, it simply didn't matter how I tried moving closer to Jesus, I seemed just to wander in circles. Day after day He felt far away, even though the Bible reminded me that He's "very near."[2]

My faith had become stuck. I mean really *stuck*.

I even began to doubt my salvation.

"Daddy, will you get to be with Jesus in heaven?" my young son asked one Sunday morning at the breakfast table.

I dropped a box of frosted cereal and gazed at him blankly. Suddenly I couldn't get any words out. As I hesitated, a simple but substantial question from the mouth of a child seemed to hang in the air forever.

Christopher stared back with his perfect six-year-old face—messy blond hair, blue eyes, freckled nose. His expression was so innocent, so trusting.

I remained speechless. Eventually I blurted: "I think so. I mean, yes—of course, I'm going to heaven." I nervously scooped up the sugary bits and nodded.

"Good," he replied, "because I want to be there with you."

My heart melted. *What IS my problem? What's with all this doubt? God is real. I committed my life to Him—will spend eternity with Him. How I feel right now doesn't matter . . . emotions aren't infallible. End of discussion.*

A few hours later I slipped into church mode as if nothing were wrong. I switched on my social grin, shook one hand after another, and toed the line of my Sunday Script, jabbering in Christianese and fronting upbeat body language with well-timed gestures.

"Michael!" A familiar voice rose above the crowd. I turned and locked eyes with a friend.

"Lance!" I exclaimed cheerfully. "Man, it's good to see you."

Now I wasn't acting. We'd been getting to know each other; things were clicking. We were both crazy in love with our wives; we enjoyed being dads; I'd also sensed right away that this guy was no spiritual wimp. Genuine, easygoing, blunt, with just a hint of "warrior grit"—as a kid, Lance probably was the boy who'd bloody your nose, then give you a ride home on his bike.[3]

"How's life these days?" he asked with a handshake. He looked me directly in the eye.

My conscience kicked in: *Go on—open up. Get past the surface. Maybe ask when you can meet for coffee . . .*

But after pausing, I brightened my grin. "I'm . . . good. Yeah, life's really, uh . . . *good*. You?"

"I'm good too. How's the family?"

"Good. All good. Just dropped off my boy in children's church; my wife's waiting for me over there." (I waved.) "Things couldn't be better. Beautiful day outside; can't wait to enjoy some sunshine later." Inwardly, I groaned. *I'm pathetic—a habitual liar or a repressed actor. Maybe both.*

"Well, then, what can I say but . . . *good*?!" Lance winked and glanced at his watch. "Catch you inside, okay? I've got to find my family."

I nodded and resumed pressing through the crowded hall. A few steps past the missions table, a few steps from the sanctuary, three piercing words stopped me in my tracks: *Quit being phony.*

I glanced over my shoulder to be certain Lance hadn't said it. At that moment, my head flooded with hard-to-admit thoughts:

Busy, worn-out, directionless—your spiritual life needs attention.

Where's your warrior grit? Your nose hasn't been bloodied lately. You're playing it safe these days—have you forgotten that life, faith, isn't about avoiding risk? Somewhere along the way you've stopped trusting.

Don't you remember how much God loves you? The Creator, the Savior—He made you, He knows you, and your life matters. You have a greater purpose than you could ever imagine.

Take your eyes off dead things—it's time to start living again.

I slid through the maze and found my wife already settled into worship. I was utterly distracted. An acid-like taste crept up into my throat, reminding me that despite all the happy talk so easily and consistently rolling off my lips, my life was far from vital. I felt spiritually extinguished.

God hadn't gone anywhere during my desert wanderings— I had. That day He was whispering, shouting, touching, and tugging at my heart. Maybe there had been a thousand steps between us . . . but it was down to just one.

I had a choice to make.

Spiritual Nosedives and Silent Killers

No Christ-follower is immune to spiritual burnout, and there's no Christ-follower who always sees it coming. While there's much to be learned in such a time, we cannot afford to ignore our status or refuse to face up—prolonged inattention is soul-killing if we bury reality and keep pretending. What's truly daunting is that most of us don't realize this is happening even *as it happens.*

We get caught up in our own agendas. So much of our time already is devoted to our responsibilities and commitments that when we do have the opportunity to seek real recharge and rejuvenation, we tend to busy ourselves with habits and hobbies that distract and amuse without refueling us. We become more and more self-absorbed, apathetic toward others, inauthentic in speech and prayer. We stay busy *being busy*: increasingly, almost all our energy and other resources are earmarked toward keeping ourselves afloat on the unreliable buoyancy of our own wants and needs.

At some point, we're startled to realize we've lost sight of the One we claim to be following—the One we say has saved us, is reshaping us, will sustain us. Panic threatens to take over; we know we can't continue on this path and that we have to confront the situation we've allowed ourselves to accept. And at that critical moment we face a choice: Start living again by taking a step in a different direction, or stay comfortable on the present path and watch more and more life being sapped from our souls. (Seasons of barrenness can plague us through *spiritual burnout*—when our faith seems empty and meaningless, often because we've taken God out of the picture—and in *spiritual deserts*, when our conversation with the Lord seems stifled or silent and we feel we can't sense His presence or discern His voice.)

I like how Frank Laubach describes the awakening experience:

> Has God ever struck you as the *Great Stirrer-Up*? One thing He seems to have determined is that we shall not fall asleep. We make or discover paradises for ourselves, and these paradises begin to lull us into sleepy satisfaction. Then God comes with His awakening hand, takes us by the shoulders and gives us a thorough awakening.
>
> And God knows we need it. If our destiny is to *grow* on and on and on, into some far more beautiful creatures than we are now, with more of the ideals of Christ, that means that we need to have the shells broken quite frequently so that we can grow.[4]

Most of us have great difficulty acknowledging that our faith journey will take us through the soul's many changing conditions. "We may not have expected things to get tougher before they get better," Howard Baker points out. "Certainly, we did not expect to have our innermost selves exposed—our misgivings about God, our doubt, apathy, disillusionment, depression."[5]

Too often we think as though we already were supposed to "have arrived." A. W. Tozer noted that for many believers,

> Everything is made to center upon the initial act of "accepting" Christ, and we are not expected thereafter to crave any further revelation of God to our souls. We have been snared in the coils of a spurious logic which insists that if we have found Him, we need no more seek Him.[6]

Many believers act as if they have it all together even though they're bogged down with fear and doubt, riddled with sin. Most Christ-followers need some real clues on how to win the day spiritually and get unstuck.

Maybe you're among them. I certainly am.

A Closer Look at What Holds Us Back

"I'm too busy."

I have a husband and three boys to look after, as well as a coffee shop to run. I'm up by four every morning, opening our business, preparing food for the day, briefing the staff . . . then I pull on my mom hat and get my family out the door. By evening—after my kids have been shuffled between music lessons, chess club, karate classes—I'm so exhausted the only thing I can do is collapse into bed. I barely have time to cook, bathe, pay bills—and do the hundreds of other things I'm supposed to get done in a given day.

Bible-reading, prayer, "doing things" to draw me closer to Christ? I often neglect these, and it makes me bitter inside. I get so stressed and full of worry. I'm tired all the time. I want

things to be different, but I just don't know where to begin . . .
and I don't have enough hours in the day. *(Julie, 44, Santa Fe)*

"I keep falling into the same temptations."

I've lost so much sleep over this in the past few months. I feel
sick and twisted and dirty. I'm literally torn up inside—so
full of shame, guilt, and confusion.

How could I let this happen? Why am I attracted to something so dark? I'd give anything to go back and change my
actions. Yet I can't stop doing what I know is wrong. I feel
trapped, alone—stuck.

I'm a Christ-follower, so I know pornography is wrong.
I've prayed and cried—yet I just can't seem to let go of my
unthinkable desires. I don't want to hurt myself and others,
and I'm dying spiritually. What I do in secret has to stop, but
I don't know how. I'm writing these words in the middle of
the night. I feel so ashamed. O Lord, *please, please* help me
through this spiritual battle. I don't want to be destroyed.
I want to overcome . . . and win. I desperately need hope,
courage, and strength. *(Josh, 19, Chicago)*

"I don't understand the Bible."

I'm a little ashamed to admit it, but I have a Bible in just
about every room of my house yet rarely take the time to
read any of them. And even though I've been a Christian
since my teen years, I don't really understand what the Bible
is and what it's for. I certainly don't know how to apply the
Scriptures to my life.

People refer to this book as *God's Living Word*. Friends
at church tell me to "eat" the Scriptures daily. I'm not sure
how to do this. And, frankly, I think the writing can be hard
to understand. . . . If I'm supposed to treat it like food—
mentally chewing on each word as I read—I find these pages
hard to digest. I don't mean to sound irreverent, that's just
how it is for me.

My wife, on the other hand, is amazing. I'm struggling to eat a sandwich of wheat bread and mustard, with a little meat in the middle—in other words, Christian books and other inspirational writings with a slice of the Bible mixed in. But she's across the room chewing on raw meat, tearing it up and loving it. She spends a lot of time in the Bible, and that really inspires me.

How can I become more like her? I want a more meaningful time in the Scriptures. But how? *(Kevin, 47, Fairfax, VA)*

"I'm petrified about the future."

I had dreams of one day starring on Broadway. I love dancing and acting. Yet I sensed God telling me, "What would happen if you gave those dreams to Me—and I didn't give them back to you?"

I thought, *Are you joking?* But I just couldn't deny it: In my heart I knew He was telling me to quit theater.

I went through a time of actually hating God and thinking Him so cruel for wanting to take away my desires. Yet the more I resisted the more miserable I felt. And during this struggle, I fell down some stairs and was diagnosed with a disease called reflex sympathetic dystrophy (RSD). Doctors said I'd never again walk normally, that I'd end up in a wheelchair. Everything was taken away in two days—my dreams of dance, of Broadway. Now this young woman who'd been a "good little church girl" most of her life was struggling with her faith and unsure if she wanted to follow God at all. *(Alyssa, 24, Nashville)*

The Other Side of the Door

The above are just a few reasons Christians give for neglecting their faith and ignoring the Bible. Ironic, isn't it—you'd think we'd draw closer to God for help with our countless struggles.

Instead, many of us limp along, frustrated, lonely, stuck . . . forgetting what God promises, what's within our reach.

How about you? You've heard part of our stories and glanced at spiritual snapshots of others. At times you likewise have yearned for intimacy with your Creator—wanting to know Him, needing the assurance of being known by Him. What's holding you back? Are the stresses of daily life coming between you and God? Are you paralyzed by doubt? Sin? Past wounds?

I recall feeling I was on the outside of the world, *the wrong side of the door.* What I needed was just ahead . . . just *out* of reach. This is how C. S. Lewis spoke of humankind's spiritual longing:

> We discern the freshness and purity of morning, but they do not make us fresh and pure. We cannot mingle with the splendours we see. But all the leaves of the New Testament are rustling with the rumour that it will not always be so. Someday, God willing, we shall get in.[7]

I desperately want in. I hope you do too. (In chapter 7 I'll share more about my struggles and about what's helping me to thrive again.)

Moving Toward *Relationship*

"Catch on fire with enthusiasm, and people will come for miles to watch you burn."[8]

Blunt words that shock the ears, yet to John Wesley this was the *only* way to experience life as a Christ-follower.

Wesley, an Oxford scholar, crisscrossed Britain (and elsewhere) until ultimately he'd traversed more than 250,000 miles in an era when horses were his best mobility. This minister shared the gospel with fire and passion in open-air sanctuaries, and everywhere he went—from factory yards to town squares—he drew a crowd. His mission was to awaken a sleepy church.

"He [God] is continually saying to every child of man: 'My son, give Me thy heart!' And to give our hearts to any other is plain idolatry. Accordingly, whatever takes our heart from Him, or shares it with Him, is an idol."[9]

Wesley knew this from experience. His own heart had remained caught up in idolatry, even after he'd identified himself with Christ. Eventually, he testified of his heart being "strangely warmed"[10] and revived.

But that didn't occur until after his brush with death.

In 1738, Wesley was sailing home to England after a transatlantic journey to Georgia. Not only had he felt ineffective evangelistically, what's more, he couldn't help feeling that something was profoundly lacking in his own faith. He later wrote, "I went to America to convert the Indians, but, oh, who shall convert me?"[11]

He'd been feeling very small against the endless ocean and infinite sky when suddenly *BOOM!*—a thunderclap and a lightning bolt. Then a few chilly droplets turned into an all-out downpour.

Before long, mountainous waves rose around the tiny ship, jetting it skyward toward the clouds and plunging it deep into churning canyons. Violent swells turned the formerly peaceful waters into a deadly, ruthless explosion of assault.

Wesley, panicked as he watched, headed belowdecks and began to pray: "O God in heaven, I fear we may not make it. I fear this may be the end. But I'm not ready to die. In fact, I fear death."[12]

When he looked up, his eyes focused on a curious group of passengers—members of an order called the Moravian Brethren. Despite the chaos outside and all around, these people were calmly projecting an amazing peace.

46

I must have what they've found, he vowed silently.

Several weeks later, with the nightmare behind him, Wesley visited a Moravian Society meeting and discovered what he'd been missing. He placed complete trust in Jesus Christ as his Lord and Savior, receiving the assurance of complete forgiveness and the guarantee of eternal life in heaven.

In that little building, after years spent pursuing not relationship but religion, John Wesley came to know the experience of a genuine conversion. His heart was set ablaze by the Living God. He wrote in his journal:

> *In the evening I went very unwillingly to a society in Aldersgate Street, where one was reading Luther's preface to the Epistle to the Romans. About a quarter before nine, while he was describing the change, which God works in the heart through faith in Christ, I felt my heart strangely warmed. I felt I did trust in Christ, Christ alone, for my salvation; and an assurance was given me that He had taken away my sins, even mine, and saved me from the law of sin and death.*[13]

Is Your Heart "Strangely Warmed"?

Wesley hungered to know God intimately. During his youth he'd committed himself to prayer and study, yearning to "draw ever closer to Jesus." Yet despite all his good efforts, like many in the same circumstances, he left out one crucial element of faith: *relationship.*

For much of his early Christian walk, Wesley was concerned with following "spiritual rules" and attaining head knowledge. What's more, he hadn't thoroughly trusted Jesus or comprehended what God's grace was all about. He'd allowed his life to be filled with distractions, what he called *idols*: other people, as well as his pride, reputation, and accomplishments. His will versus God's.

Did you realize an idol can be a person, a pursuit—anything that takes priority over Jesus? If we don't allow the Lord to direct our lives, we can end up worshiping false gods without even comprehending it.

What rules your life? What's holding you back? Are you learning to trust Christ . . . and to take a step of faith with Him every day?

Do you yearn for spiritual intimacy with Jesus—for a heart set ablaze?

———

Let's briefly revisit the story of Alyssa, who amid great trauma was in a crisis of faith, so frightened about the future that she wondered whether she even wanted to follow God, much less grow closer to Him. But . . .

Then it happened: a miracle. God began to change my heart—and mend my body. I slowly regained full ability to walk. Suddenly my lifelong dream didn't seem so important. I began to realize that His call on my life wasn't to be an actress or to play a role. God wanted me to be real with Him and with myself. He asked me to trust Him with everything, including my career.

Little by little, God began to stir a passion for serving Him through a music ministry. I didn't know how life was going to turn out—whether I'd serve Him on the mission field or in a church. But I knew I had a purpose—His purpose.

Still, I must be honest: My struggles aren't over. Despite all I've come through, I'm still learning what it means to surrender my life to Jesus—my dreams, my hopes, my stubborn will. At times I feel petrified about the future. At times I still pull away from the Lord and try to go in my own direction.

I'm glad God is patient and won't ever give up on me.

———◉———

It's a strange paradox: The bestselling book of all time—the Holy Bible—also is the *most misunderstood, least agreed upon,* and relative to the number of copies owned, perhaps *least read* resource. How can this be? In the next chapter, Arnie looks at why a staggering number of us don't grasp what the Bible is for, why we open it "on occasion," and why we're clueless about basic scriptural teachings and truths.

———◉———

Research Reveals: Christians grow through *relationship,* not religion. We stall when we focus on impersonal formulas and empty habits.

Encouraging Nudge: Nearly every believer has felt separated from God, yet He's "very near."[14] His Word is true, no matter what emotions suggest. It's a bumpy ride through life if we persist in succumbing to feelings, which can change like the wind. But ignoring our inner state is unwise, for as sensations from physical nerve endings alert us to outer conditions, so our soul status often indicates how we need to pay attention and thus understand how God is guiding our lives.[15]

Take a look at unstuck.gotandem.com for more practical ways to grow spiritually. Do this every day during your forty-five-day journey.

Spiritual
Stepping Stones

● **DAY 4**

Scripture to Remember: John 15:12–17

Question to Consider: For whom would I "lay down my life"? (Spend some time reflecting on your answer.)

DAY 5

Scripture to Remember: Mark 12:28–34

Question to Consider: What does it mean to love God with all my heart, soul, mind, and strength?

DAY 6

Scripture to Remember: Isaiah 43:1–2

Question to Consider: Do I believe that God has summoned me by name—and that He will be with me when I feel spiritually lost? (Why, or why not?)

three

The Bestseller
Many Won't Read

It's not those parts of the Bible I don't understand that scare
me. It's those parts I do understand.

—Mark Twain

Despite doing "religious things" during my youth—attending
Christian schools, darkening my church's doors each Sunday
morning and evening, showing up at Wednesday night prayer
meetings—I (Arnie) found myself relating to Mark Twain.

The Bible "parts" drilled into me were endless rules. The
whole thing had become *The Book of NO!* And the older
I got, the more it seemed Scripture bashed all things *fun*.
Simply stated, I didn't know what the Bible was, and I had
the wrong idea of what the Bible was for.

I thought of Jesus as the guy who'd save me from going
to hell, and several times I'd made a choice to follow Him.
When someone told me, "God has a wonderful plan for your
life," I agreed wholeheartedly; I'd even memorized the passage

that promises "all things working together for good—if you believe in Jesus." (Flip open your Bible and read Romans 8:28–30 very closely. Note that the words aren't exactly what I'd memorized! Verse 28 reads, "We know that in all things God works for the good of those who love him, who have been called according to his purpose.")

Yet at no time during all those training years did anyone tell me God talks to us through His Word. For the life of me, I thought a relationship with Him was based on spoken prayer. More specifically, I thought it boiled down to our asking God for things . . . and His making things happen. *God actually and personally communicating with me through the Bible* was utterly foreign to me.

Looking back, I had a relationship based on a *decision* to believe in Jesus. And in all honesty my friendship with God was pretty much a one-way deal. I even thought prayer tapped into something magical in the spiritual world. *We speak to God; maybe He talks back to us through our feelings.* It made enough sense to me, as it does to so many.

What difference *does* the Bible, in fact, make?

In secular research, the assumption is that it has no impact at all. As a new believer, though, I noticed that among those claiming to be Christ-followers, some truly were ablaze for the Lord, growing spiritually in leaps and bounds. I wondered why. And I wondered how.

What Got Me Started

Brick-and-mortar bookstores have lined their shelves with almost countless renderings of Scripture: sizes and colors and styles and editions. Online are even more selections: illustrated versions, audio with dramatic twists, apps in dozens of translations for PCs, Macs, smartphones, e-readers—there are myriad options via nearly every medium, yet, once again, humankind's bestselling book is its *most misunderstood, least agreed upon,* and relative to the number of copies owned, perhaps *least read* resource.

How can this be?

Another eye-opener: American Christians own multiple copies (five per household, on average), but a staggering number of believers don't grasp what the Bible is for, read it only "on occasion," and are ignorant of basic scriptural teachings and truths.

WHY?

Why all the confusion?

Why is Scripture so accessible, yet so neglected?

Why should we care?

After all, in what ways can a collection of ancient sources reliably speak to twenty-first-century issues? And why do many messages seem impractical, hard to follow? There's politically incorrect language that offends some as well, and it's not always immediately obvious how customs or laws of the time do or don't connect with what's necessary for us now.[1]

Since Christianity is all about an intimate, personal relationship with Christ—not just a bunch of doctrines to believe or sins to avoid—how does the Bible relate to spiritual growth? How much do we need Scripture if we already pray, worship, and connect with a community of believers?

My quest for answers started when I began working with Dr. Woodrow Kroll, who explained to me his concern for biblically illiterate Christians (he'd been monitoring the issue for more than twenty-six years). He believed it was the number-one problem facing the church in America and getting worse each year. At first I thought, *What honest difference does it make who knows whose brother-in-law ruled some tribe thousands of years ago? Does scoring high on "Jeopardy for Christians" mean we're better people?*

Kroll went on to explain that Bible illiteracy isn't only a head thing—many Christ-followers are starving spiritually because we simply don't know God's Word. He gave me a challenge: *Why do so many Americans own several copies of the Bible when they rarely read them? What difference* does *the Bible make in the life of the Christian?*

Six years ago I launched a massive study. I wondered if I could observe noticeable differences in people's lives. What impact, if any, did various actions and commitments and endeavors have on one's spiritual life?

Professionally, I'm a behaviorist, which means I study people's actions and responses to environmental stimuli. I like to figure out why people do what they do, and when beneficial to their well-being, I like to help determine how their behaviors can be modified. Unlike a psychologist who might hand you a box of tissues and encourage you to spill every emotion you've had since kindergarten, I work with observable and quantifiable processes. It's something like working with people that medical science can't appreciably assist; my job enters in with "Whether or not you can *get* better, you certainly can *do* better."

Put simply, I spend many late nights and early mornings sifting through raw data about human actions, analyzing responses to surveys, building statistical models, testing hypotheses—and connecting a whole bunch of "behavior dots," so to speak. I gather my data through carefully constructed questionnaires and interviews. (Yes, I used to wear thick-framed glasses; but no, I don't own a pocket protector.)

When I applied these methods to research about Scripture engagement as it relates to behavior and spiritual life, here's what I learned: The Bible matters—a lot. In fact, *spiritually and behaviorally speaking, we found that nothing comes close to having the Bible's impact on the spiritual lives of those who engage it.*

Engaging God's Word consistently makes *the* difference in regard to lasting spiritual growth—especially in the realms of overcoming temptations and changing negative behaviors (overcoming past wounds, addictions, etc.). As for the puzzling disconnect between believers and Bible reading, I uncovered 11,000 excuses for neglecting God's Word. I also heard thousands more reasons why people *do* read the Bible—and about the powerful ways in which it has changed their lives.

Faith and the Bible: Seventy Thousand Voices Tell All

I'll unveil the research in bits and pieces throughout this book. If you love details, don't miss appendix 2, "Our Research Methods." The bottom line: Since 2005, my team at the Center for Bible Engagement (CBE) has studied the spiritual lives of more than seventy thousand Americans. We've examined the faith habits of young and old alike; people representing a variety of races, economic backgrounds, and faith experiences—including Christ-followers and non-Christians. We're investigating religious preferences and beliefs, how people communicate with God, ways believers grow spiritually, church affiliation and attendance, frequency and perceived effectiveness of prayer, daily temptations faced, risks taken, moral behaviors, Bible-reading habits, and how God's Word applies to all these factors.

Our data come from Internet-based surveys, both random samples of the general population and non-random samples of self-identified Christians. I don't want to parrot legalese (like what comes with credit card offers and pharmaceutical claims), but I want to emphasize three important points:

(1) our findings are free of CBE opinions and personal biases; (2) our analyses are reliable because they've been replicated across so many different studies; and (3) we constructed statistical models to test what we've observed.

We're gradually piecing together an accurate picture of present-day American spirituality, and we now have scientific evidence for the power of Bible engagement. Here are some key findings uncovered to date.

Our lives are dramatically different when we're engaged with Scripture four or more times a week.

There are significant differences in the moral behaviors and spiritual maturity of believers who read or listen to the Bible at least four times a week compared to those who read or hear Scripture less often or never at all. In fact, such engagement motivates service for God and impacts the world for Him (through helping in church, loving the unlovely, reaching out to the needy).

This finding alone is truly groundbreaking! *The Bible changes our lives.* We can be radically better (actually strengthened and renewed) if we allow God to speak to us through His Word—that is, if we listen to Him through what He says and ponder what it means.

Getting "Powered by Four" is key.[2] There are no statistical differences in the behaviors of those who read/listen to the Bible one to three times weekly and those who spend zero days doing so. That is, the lives of Christians who rarely read the Bible appear identical to those who don't follow Christ at all.

We must engage the Bible four or more times a week—*receiving* God's Word, *reflecting* on God's Word, *responding* to God's Word. For one thing, when we're engaged in it, the growth we experience builds a protective factor within us. Specifically, for example, we're less likely to take part in negative and soul-robbing behaviors, like viewing pornography, abusing drugs, giving in to drunkenness, and engaging in sex outside of marriage.

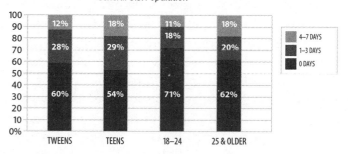

DAYS PER WEEK READING OR LISTENING TO THE BIBLE
General U.S. Population

Those who invest in the Bible are in the minority.

Despite the power of Bible engagement, in a given week most Americans don't hear from God at all—or at least consistently—through His Word.

This includes Christ-followers. Among believers we surveyed, only about 25 percent of tweens and about 40 percent of teens, young adults, and people twenty-five and older currently, consistently turn to God's Word for spiritual growth and daily direction.

It's no secret: The Christian church is neglecting God's Word.

A disconnection from God's Word is the primary reason Christ-followers are losing the day in droves.

Common sense shows that biblically illiterate churchgoers are spiritually immature and vulnerable to anti-Christian teachings and doctrines. Without a firm grasp of the Bible that's nurtured through daily engagement, believers are less able to stand strong in the faith they claim, less confident in telling others about Christ, and often too weak to withstand the temptations they encounter. Our findings prove these assumptions.

What kinds of things are we falling for? The same stuff that has plagued believers for centuries, with a few variations; for example, there isn't much new about hedonism, relativism, entitlement-based ethics, essentially pagan practices of a million stripes, or even "prosperity theology." (Addressing these is far beyond the scope of this work, but Google some of these if you want to learn more regarding what they're about. Consider the number of times these and other concepts have collided with your life or the life of someone you love.)

Current findings by leading researchers (including the Pew Research Center and the Barna Research Group) have revealed disheartening trends. Our research not only supports those conclusions but also connects the dots and uncovers the trends' source: Bible illiteracy. Neglecting God's Word is the main reason believers become stuck spiritually, get disconnected from God, and are prone to losing ground to all kinds of damaging thoughts and harmful behaviors.

Current Drifts Among Christ-Followers

- *Pornography is tripping up Christian men.* Men attending church who occasionally indulge in it: 53 percent.[3] Overall, the largest consumers of Internet porn: men between twenty-five and forty-four (46 percent).[4]
- *Unmarried Christians are living together.* A significant minority of self-identified born-again Christians, particularly those under thirty-five, has cohabited (and many see nothing wrong with it).

- *Marriages are failing among believers.* Divorce rates for Christians are statistically identical to those of non-Christians (32 percent vs. 33 percent, respectively).[5]
- *Adults are leaving Christian churches.* More than one-fourth of American adults have left the faith in which they were raised for another religion or no religion at all.[6] (Some attempt to keep the faith but reject "church.")
- *A growing number of men are lukewarm.* Men (about one in five) are more likely than women (about one in eight) to claim no formal religious affiliation.[7]
- *A significant number of young adults have left the Christian church.* Among Americans eighteen to twenty-nine, one in four say they're not currently affiliated with any particular faith.[8]

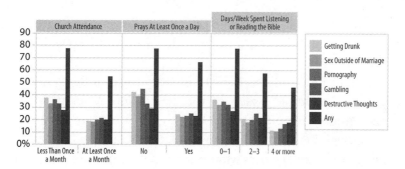

SPIRITUAL DISCIPLINES AND RISK BEHAVIORS

I'm sure that, like me, you're dealing with your own struggles—maybe a few things on that list (and/or others). Maybe you're fried on "traditional religion." Maybe you hold the Bible to be God's inspired and trustworthy Word but have trouble getting into it. (If so, this book isn't about guilt; instead, let's find some answers together.)

If you're among those who leave the Scriptures on a shelf, what holds you back? People mention all kinds of things—lack of time, confusion over what God's Word is, lack of knowledge as to how He intends us to read it. Some point to "worldly distractions" (work, materialism, pressures) and the hypocrisy they see in believers as stumbling blocks. Various media and many pop culture voices have contributed to the uncertainty and bewilderment.

I'm not surprised by any of these excuses—especially the last two.

Conflicting Opinions: Is the Media Helping or Hurting?

Our nation's growing ignorance of basic Bible teachings scored some laughs one night on NBC's *Tonight Show with Jay Leno*. As the silver-haired host circulated through his audience he sought responses to statements like "Name one of the Ten Commandments."

"God helps those who help themselves," someone ventured.

With raised eyebrows, Leno said, "Name one of the apostles." *No one could.*

Finally he asked the crowd to identify the four Beatles. The answers rolled off dozens of tongues: "George, Paul, John, and Ringo!" people shouted.[9]

Though Leno was joking around, this absurdity (no laughing matter) underscores what our research confirms: America is on the verge of becoming post-biblical. While jests shed some light on a growing problem, other media personalities actually have added to it. Case in point: *O'Reilly vs. Maher.*

A nationally televised debate between cable's king of conservative commentary and an accomplished comedian (and HBO host) who claims to be a "liberal voice of sanity," the battle of the Bills played out on the Fox News Channel. Bill

O'Reilly intended to be a voice for Christianity, while Bill Maher would represent an atheist's viewpoint.

Maher threw one punch by insisting that "faith is the purposeful suspension of critical thinking," and asking, "If your perfect holy book is written by God, why is there stuff in there that makes no sense?"

O'Reilly rolled his eyes, flashed his trademark sneer, and then rebutted. What he said made some viewers even more confused than ever: "It's allegorical," he countered, "designed to teach a greater truth that apparently has eluded you."[10]

Really? The Bible is largely or entirely figurative and symbolic?

Maher noted some stories he could swallow only were he to "suspend reality." Are these just tales invented to teach lessons, or did they happen?

> Noah, who lived 950 years, built a big boat, filled it with lions and hippos (and countless other critters), survived global destruction . . . and then started the planet's repopulation.[11]

> With his hand stretched out over the sea, Moses tapped God's power and parted the water so the Israelites could walk across.[12]

> Jonah tried to sail away from God, but got swallowed by a massive fish. He survived inside for three days and nights, then prayed for God's help, was vomited onto dry land, and did as God instructed.[13]

After the show, websites buzzed with reactions. Here's how one blogger summed up the segment:

> This interview is more evidence that we Christians need to speak clearly and succinctly about the basics of Christianity

and what the Bible is to Christians. Atheists . . . are listening; they are reading. We need deeper commitment and due diligence in reaching our young people and adults. We need to have our facts straight. . . . Life is confusing enough without all the popular talking heads on television spreading fallacies about the Bible and our Lord.[14]

Differing "Perspectives"

Exactly what *is* this thick book many intend to read but neglect because there "aren't enough hours" in the day? Ask twenty different people and end up with twenty different answers—even within Christian circles.

Gone are the days when most Christ-followers knew Bible basics (e.g., naming the Ten Commandments, or identifying the apostles). Gone are the days when they could articulate how *most* Christian churches view Scripture: "a message inspired by the Holy Spirit"; "divine revelation"; "trusted, timeless, and relevant instruction for all believers"; "*the* voice of authority."

The face of Christianity is being changed by believers disillusioned with the "institutional" church and who advocate "deconstruction" of worship and community—for example, people who identify with the emerging church (or the emergent movement). They're part of more than 58 million Americans who make up two generational segments of our society: "Mosaics" (born between 1984 and 2002) and "Busters" (born between 1965 and 1983). Christians of these generations are among those often most skeptical of present-day Christianity.[15] Many don't view the Bible as the Almighty's authoritative words. They see Scripture and the Christian tradition as a whole, from an historical, metaphorical, and sacramental perspective.[16]

Let's look at some perspectives. Here, various Christians— prominent and unknown, outspoken and ordinary—tell what the Bible means to them. As you read their comments, think about how you'd weigh in on this discussion. (*Note:* Not all of these are oppositional.)

That the Bible Is God's Trustworthy, Authoritative Word

Millions of people today are searching for a reliable voice of authority. The Word of God is the only real authority we have. His Word sheds light on human nature, world problems and human suffering. But beyond that, it clearly reveals the way to God. . . . When we read God's Word, we fill our hearts with His words, and God is speaking to us.[17]

Billy Graham

That the Bible Should Be Taken Seriously but Not Literally

I see the Bible as a human response to God. Rather than seeing God as Scripture's ultimate author, I see the Bible as the response of these two ancient communities [ancient Israel and the early Christian movement] to their experience of God. As such, it contains their stories of God, their perceptions of God's character and will, their prayers to and praise of God, their perceptions of the human condition and the paths of deliverance, their religious and ethical practices, and their understanding of what faithfulness to God involves. As the product of these two communities, the Bible thus tells us about how *they* saw things, not about how *God* sees things.[18]

Marcus J. Borg

That the Bible's Supernatural Element Sets It Apart

When we read it, the Bible opens us up. It reads us. It searches us in the deepest way possible. It reveals our hearts and motivations. It convicts and comforts us. When we read it, the

Holy Spirit confirms in our hearts that it is not the word of men but the very Word of God himself. They are words unlike any other words on earth. They are true and eternal. . . . God honors those who revere and respect Him and His Word— those who treat Scripture not as mere words on a page or human invention but as the holy, God-breathed, powerful, and authoritative words of the Almighty.[19]

Joshua Harris

That God's Word Brings Us Into Intimacy With Him

The Bible was written so that anyone who wants to know who God is and how they are to live in a way that pleases Him can read it and find out. . . . The Bible tells us everything we need to know about life. That, my friend, is why you need to study it for yourself. . . . When you know what God says, what He means, and how to put His truths into practice, you will be equipped for every circumstance of life. Through a diligent study of God's Word, under the guidance of His Spirit, you'll drop a strong anchor that will hold in the storms of life. You will know your God.[20]

Kay Arthur

That God Is a Person; the Bible Is Paper

God existed before the Bible existed; God exists independently of the Bible now. God is a person; the Bible is paper. God gave us this papered Bible to lead us to love His person. But the person and the paper are not the same.[21]

Scot McKnight

That the Scriptures Reveal God's Story

The Bible is one book, one history, one story, His story. Behind ten thousand events stands God, the builder of history, the maker of the ages. Eternity bounds the one side, eternity bounds the other side, and time is in between: Genesis—origins, Revelation—endings, and all the way between, God is working things out. You can go down into the minutest detail everywhere and see that there is one great purpose moving through the ages: the eternal design of the almighty God to redeem a wrecked and ruined world.[22]

Henrietta C. Mears

That the Bible Tells Us "Why," Not "How"

The problem Christians face is that the Bible is not attempting to answer "how" questions. And if it is, it's a terribly written book and not practical in any way in terms of addressing how to succeed, how to get married, how to be more sexy, how to lose weight, how to organize your finances or how to build a business. Instead, the Bible is a "why" book. The Bible is answering much larger questions: Why do we exist, why do we not feel loved, why is there pain in the world, why has God left us and so forth. Are there exceptions? Sure. The Proverbs has some wisdom on how to live, and there are other examples, but they are few. . . . So what does the Bible say to the average American? Among other things, it says this: You are asking the wrong questions.[23]

Donald Miller

That the Bible Isn't a Weapon to Be Used Against People

I grew up being taught that the Bible was an answer book, supplying exactly the kind of information modern Western, moderately educated people want from a phone book, encyclopedia, or legal constitution. . . . We wanted a simple, clear, efficient, and convenient plan for getting to heaven after death. Between now and then, we wanted clear assurance that God didn't like the people we didn't like, and for the same reasons we didn't like them . . . [and] a rule book that made it objectively clear, with no subjective ambiguity, what behaviors were right and wrong for all time, in all places, and among all cultures, especially if those rules confirmed our views and not those of people we considered "liberal." Although I was taught that the Bible fulfilled these modern-Western-moderately educated desires, I no longer see the Bible this way.[24]

Brian D. McLaren

What Seems Unbelievable Is Absolutely True

Having dedicated my life to research for the church, I'm absolutely thrilled that we've shown engaging God's Word consistently makes *the* difference when it comes to lasting spiritual growth.

Even so, you might say, *"How can you prove faith?" God and His ways are to be trusted and believed. Besides, the power of the Bible is no secret. That's what makes it supernatural.*

I can't agree more.

Lab tests and mathematical formulas won't change hearts *or* prove the supernatural power of God's Word. Engaging the Bible and hearing the Lord's voice through it must be experienced personally. To be blunt, it really doesn't matter what a stubborn, arrogant, self-centered human thinks anyway, right? Truth is truth. Regardless of what we affirm or deny, God *is* all-knowing, everywhere present, the Creator of all things, the everlasting Ruler of heaven and earth.

And thankfully for our sake, God is love.

He made us in His image, and after we've stubbornly, arrogantly rejected Him to pursue sin (self-centeredness), He pursues us with incomprehensible passion to the moment of our very last breath. God loves you and me so much, He walked in our steps, wearing skin and feeling what we feel,

---

Why Some Believers Don't Read the Bible

The top two (out of 11,000) reasons for not reading God's Word are "I'm too busy" and "I don't have enough time." In a typical workday, the average adult American spends

- 1 hour eating and drinking
- 8.8 hours working (includes e-mailing, web surfing, texting/messaging, phone calls during work hours)
- 1.3 hours caring for others (includes children)
- 1 hour on household activities (includes cooking and cleaning)
- 1.7 hours on "other" activities (includes personal time spent online, texting/messaging, phone calls)
- 2.6 hours in leisure activities (includes TV)
- 7.6 hours sleeping[25]

---

and then took our sin to the cross, giving His own life to offer us eternal life with Him.

That's why I'm applying science to faith.

I want to be used by God to open hearts and minds to the truth. I want to help burned-out, spiritually stuck Christ-followers to get unstuck—to show how spiritual losers like me can start winning battles and carrying the day.

I'm telling you: *Bible engagement is the key.*

The changes won't happen in a flash, and Bible engagement isn't about axioms or theorems that pledge a "healthier, wealthier, wiser new you."

But engaging God's Word *will* change you.

When these truths are worked into your life consistently, you will find God speaks to you intimately and guides you uniquely.

Take Your Spiritual Temperature

Amount of time spent in the Bible may be a far better indicator of your "spiritual state" than church attendance. For Christians in particular, immersion in the Word correlates with spiritual growth, including knowledge of the Bible and a desire to share faith with others.

(Ultimately you *will* be healthier, wealthier, and wiser—whether or not in ways that the world applauds.)

Please understand this: It's not only what's written in Scripture that will get your heart pumping; it's also what happens when you let the words into your heart. No one can explain the Bible's supernatural influence and impact—it must be experienced. The more I engage God's Word and respond to what He says, the more my life is molded into what He intends it to be.

Even though I believe Scripture's worth reading for what I can learn, there's something even more exciting and worthwhile on a relational plane. God's Word gets past my head, touches my heart, and revives my soul. It renews my mind and begins to reproduce God's heart and character in my life.[26]

Next, we'll examine another factor in being spiritually stuck: *temptation.*

Research Reveals: There's a huge disconnect between what American Christians *think* about the Bible and what they *do* with it. Almost all say it's their life authority, yet just two in five have read the whole thing. Virtually all say it's relevant to their daily lives, but only half read it daily.

Encouraging Nudge: Owning a Bible and believing it to be God's inspired Word isn't enough. Forcing ourselves to read it because we should is the wrong approach too. We must engage it with our minds and our hearts. The Scriptures contain our Creator's personal message to us. Regardless of the situations we face, within its pages are hope, wisdom, direction, and the keys to getting unstuck.

Take a look at unstuck.gotandem.com for more practical ways to grow spiritually. Do this every day during your forty-five-day journey.

Spiritual
Stepping Stones

DAY 7

Scripture to Remember: Isaiah 55:8–13

Question to Consider: Do I truly care about God's thoughts and ways? If so, how can I learn more about them? If not, what's my next step?

DAY 8

Scripture to Remember: Hosea 6:1–3

Question to Consider: What must I do to return to the Lord and begin acknowledging Him again?

DAY 9

Scripture to Remember: Romans 1:18–32

Question to Consider: In what ways have I been deceived by the world? (What can I do to ensure that my mind starts being changed?)

four

From Temptation to Turmoil

God's Word to you is the same warning He gave to Cain (Genesis 4:7)—master the sin at the door of your life before it brings its inevitable and disastrous consequences. Heed His caution, and you will avoid unnecessary hardship for yourself and others.[1]

—Henry Blackaby

The year was 1972, and twelve-year-old Gene thought he'd struck gold.

Back in the deepest, darkest corner of his closet was an overstuffed cardboard box filled with treasures: comic books, slightly dog-eared baseball cards, scuffed Hot Wheels, geodes filled to bursting with beautiful crystals, aged coins, colorful marbles, and hunks of pine this California boy used to carve into rockets and missiles for his army collection.

But wrapped in a crumpled paper bag at the very bottom was something no one should own; something that had the power to own him. Gene knew deep down not to open that bag, as he had so many times before. He felt an urgency to run, to get away—and yet he also felt almost magnetically pulled toward it.

Inside the sack was Gene's secret magazine stash, and not the kinds he'd read or looked at before. These were filled with intoxicating, airbrushed photos: page after page of naked people who left nothing to the imagination. He'd gotten these from friends, who'd gotten them from older brothers.

While his mom continued talking on the phone downstairs, Gene locked his door, dug to the bottom of the box, and fished out the bag.

His pulse raced as he dumped the stuff on the floor. His eyes drank in each cover; heat filled his face. He felt like a volcano was rumbling inside. He flipped one open and gasped. Nameless bodies—people without identity or personhood— burned into his brain.

The photos bringing shame into his young soul would become harder and harder to resist. He decided to keep these "treasures" hidden; they'd be his secrets.

A Vicious Vortex

Thirty years later, Gene, a middle-aged man with his own family, had a heart paralyzed and packed with regret. *Why did I keep that load of trouble? Why did I ever start keeping secrets?*

Despite all the time that had passed, he could still recall many images he'd originally viewed. He'd also added count-less more. What began as a pull toward porn had germinated, grown, and then blown into an obsession that ran his life. It was costing him his marriage and the respect of his two children.

It all came to a head one morning.

At the breakfast table after the kids had left for school, his wife, Terri, broke his silence. "It can't go on like this, Gene. Too many unexplained late nights, too many broken promises. They need a dad, and I need a husband."

He sipped his coffee and nodded, calmly, but inside he felt his whole world falling apart. "I know . . . and I'm trying. I wish I could get unstuck from this stuff, but it's the hardest thing I've ever done. Terri, we're a completely dysfunctional family—"

"No, Gene," she corrected. "*You* are dysfunctional. Not us."

The words stung, yet he knew they were true.

Late-into-the-night cyberporn sessions were leaving him repulsed and emptier than ever. *I'm worthless—so twisted. Not an ounce of good left in me.*

Each morning he woke with his gut knotted. Despite reading a passage of Scripture and praying, shame by the ton was crushing all hope and adding layer after layer to the barrier he sensed between him and Jesus Christ.

By midday he'd feel somewhat lighter, and the slightest stimuli would churn up "mental porn shows." The smile of a pretty woman at work. Off-color conversations with the guys. *Everywhere*—TV, radio, a photo on a bus or a bench, a billboard, a magazine, a pop-up ad—the temptations seemed absolutely inescapable. By the time he'd arrive home, the act-out arc of his toxic cycle would resume and consume him all over again.

"Lord God, please take this evil away. Release me . . . help me!"

"Lord God, hear my husband's prayers. Give him strength."

"Lord God, help our dad to be a dad again."

"Lord God, heal our believing brother. Give him back his family."

Gene's family and friends didn't give up on him, remaining faithful to him, repeatedly forgiving him, continually praying for the miracle of his freedom. Eventually he had a breakthrough.

He found relief from his addictions, though the experience of getting unshackled didn't come about as he thought it would. The images still were "in his brain," the torturous pull toward temptation wasn't cutting him any slack, and he was well aware of sin crouching at his door, wanting to re-enslave him. What was changing was his relationship with Jesus.

Despite his battles against dark desires, Gene was beginning to understand that his Lord loved him more than he could possibly comprehend. (And, that nothing could change this!) In fact, the name *Savior* took on a whole new meaning. He was free to shake off his shame and approach Jesus directly. Whenever temptation sought to captivate his thoughts, he reminded himself of who was right there with him, granting him grace and giving him strength to withstand.

The change in Gene was *changing* him—and his family.

Tragically, however, after a time, this family man stumbled and fell back into addiction. Even more tragically, instead of taking up the fight, he simply gave up. In one unthinkable act, he gave away all that mattered to him, everything he'd been fighting for.

On January 26, 2010, Gene took his own life.

"Lifequakes" and Heartaches

A seemingly innocuous bit of gossip destroys an admired family's reputation.

*An envious glance grows into an unthinkable act of hatred.
A proud declaration to "stand up for my rights" topples
a community leader.*

Temptation often sways us in subtle ways. We allow our eyes to linger. We tell "a little white lie." A compromise here. A shortcut there. *Just one more drink . . . one more bite . . . one tiny "adjustment" to the ledger. . . . This is the last click. . . . No one got hurt, no one knows . . . it's no big deal.* Yet we're setting the pattern, deepening the grooves in our ruts, and, bit by bit, usually imperceptibly, the compromises expand, the shortcuts escalate, the wrong words and actions become more extreme and even more lethal. We give in more and more; more and more we become comfortable with our choices.

"And then it all came tumbling down."

Terri used those painful words to describe what had become her family's situation, and I (Arnie) can't help feeling heartbroken when I hear such stories. So many individuals, and families, feel mired in what seems like inescapable slavery. There's *no* reason it must turn out that way.

Why remain stuck and miserable when the God who saved us, the Lord we desperately want to follow, has the power to get us unstuck? Jesus Christ is reaching out to you with forgiveness, comfort, hope, freedom, strength, guidance, peace, wisdom, transformation—*real life, real answers, real faith*—exactly what you need at the very moment you need it!

Do we truly believe this?

If we do, what keeps us from accepting it?

I've mentioned that I've long analyzed people's behaviors. When I turned my attention to Gene's family, hoping to find clues to the downfall, the more I studied the more I began to see unsettling parallels between them and many other believers. A number of destructive forces at play within their lives actually are common in that they're at work in us all.

Before Gene's irreversible decision, he and Terri spoke at length with a friend about the condition of their lives. Consider the elements they emphasized:

- *Neglecting Marriage* (invested in commitments but not their relationship)
- *Losing Intimacy* ("She didn't hold my hand, she didn't initiate sex.")
- *Busy* (persistent focus on full-time careers while raising small kids)
- *Rarely Talking* ("We weren't able to communicate.")
- *Materialism* (needing "more, more . . . we picked money.")
- *Feeling Phony* (going into playacting roles)
- *Living With Secrets* (Gene started an affair.)
- *Allowing Priorities to Erode* ("We lost sight of what's important.")
- *Dysfunctional, Enslaved* ("My addiction was everywhere.")
- *Shame-Filled* ("I let her down. I went back to my addiction.")
- *Spiritually Stuck* ("I just couldn't get out of it.")
- *Out of Step With God* (They felt like they were stuck on a rapidly sinking ship.)

Consider Your Spiritual Health

Are destructive patterns showing up in your life?

Perhaps you're dealing with a strained relationship or with a struggle you can't seem to overcome. One thing is certain:

Many of us are so comfortable and materialistic—so busy with jobs, families, and churches—we go through whole seasons in which we lose sight of what's important. We end up out of alignment with God. In statistical interest, our research shows the average Christ-follower spends three months out of the year feeling lost spiritually.

Whether or not we're willing to admit it, most of us are one crisis from disaster. Are you spiritually prepared? Would a financial hardship, an illness, a broken relationship, the loss of a loved one, an unexpected temptation plunge your world into turmoil? Are you learning to trust the God who will see you through any trouble ahead—or are you clinging to a false sense of security?

Addictive processes are at work in everyone.

If you think you're immune to certain struggles, think again:

> I am not being flippant when I say that all of us suffer from addiction. Nor am I reducing the meaning of addiction. I mean in all truth that the psychological, neurological, and spiritual dynamics of full-fledged addiction are actively at work in every human being. The same processes that are responsible for addiction to alcohol and narcotics are also responsible for addiction to ideas, work, relationships, power, moods, fantasies, and an endless variety of other things. We are all addicts in every sense of the word.[2]

Dr. Gerald May says addictions are formidable foes because even though they enslave us with chains of our own making, they're beyond our control.

> Addiction also makes idolaters of us all because it forces us to worship these objects of attachment, thereby preventing

us from truly, freely loving God and one another. . . . Yet, in still another paradox, our addictions can lead us to a deep appreciation of grace. They can bring us to our knees.[3]

Temptation entices every heart.

You, me—every person on this planet—is in the heat of a war, between good and evil, being waged day after day, hour by hour. It's easy to wonder if two people live inside each body. While we yearn to be free of sin, be close to God, and grow spiritually, we find ourselves pulled toward darkness. Just when we think we've mastered a struggle, another surfaces, and we're back to doing things we don't want to do.[4] Further, and truly, the holier we strive to be the more aware we become of the battle and of our self-obsessed "dark side."

We're all born with a deadly "virus."

We're sick, which is why some refer to the Lord as the Great Physician.[5] As Christ is transforming and healing us, though, we succumb to weakness, impatience, distraction, and many of us end up doing harmful things.

This virus is *sin*.

Sin poisons our thoughts, twists our actions, and blocks us from living as we know God wants us to, living the lives for which He designed us. Sin prevents health and stifles growth, keeping our faith walk bedridden and atrophied.

There's nobody living right, not even one, nobody who knows the score, nobody alert for God. They've all taken the wrong turn; they've all wandered down blind alleys. No one's living right; I can't find a single one. Their throats are gaping graves, their tongues slick as mudslides. Every word they speak is tinged with poison. They open their mouths and pollute the air. They race for the honor of sinner-of-the-year, litter the land with heartbreak and ruin, don't know the first thing about living with others. They never give God the time of day.[6]

Sin begins with a subtle pang of temptation.

Allowed to take hold, sin can grow into a deadly "life-quake," wreaking havoc and turmoil through our choices. Jesus warned us to be on guard:

> There is nothing concealed that will not be disclosed, or hidden that will not be made known. What you have said in the dark will be heard in the daylight, and what you have whispered in the ear in the inner rooms will be proclaimed from the roofs.[7]

But here's the good news of hope: We always *have* a choice. Through Christ we can overcome temptation and reject sin.

> No temptation has overtaken you except what is common to mankind. And God is faithful; he will not let you be tempted beyond what you can bear. But when you are tempted, he will also provide a way out so that you can endure it.[8]

As we battle together, side by side, it's comforting to know we're not freaks. The sin and shame in our hearts has been shared by the godliest people who ever lived. David Wilkerson once said:

> Everything I read and heard clearly described the human condition of weakness and the ever-present struggle with evil. From Paul the apostle to church leaders such as Origen, Cyprian, Chrysostom—from Augustine to Luther, Calvin, Zwingli, Wesley, and even modern theologians and scholars—all of them described the battle and . . . admitted that they, too, were in the same struggle.[9]

What we're about to discuss is not the stuff of polite conversations, and it's not PC in any contemporary sense. We generally prefer to skip over this subject and focus on "happy" notions like "Three Short Strides to the Me I Wanna Be." Admitting our flawed-ness and our failures isn't the most enjoyable experience, but if we're to get unstuck spiritually we can't avoid it.

We're going to peer into the heart of temptation and face the obstacles that trip up Christ-followers. We'll look at how various spiritual menaces affect men and women and how they block Bible engagement (which, coincidentally, is *the best* weapon for fighting off attack and staying upright).

Temptation and Reality

"When I indulge in sinful thoughts, my ability to continue reading the Bible practically evaporates. I see that correlation now. I wish I could have understood this earlier in life."

"Temptation absolutely affects my interaction with God, and the last thing in the world I want to do is read my Bible. I usually feel this way even after I've asked for forgiveness. Why? I feel like a charlatan—as if I'm just using God. I get exhausted just thinking about how much work is ahead: There's a lot I need to do in order to become a better Christian."

"I sometimes feel like a failure and [as though] reading the Bible is a waste of time because I just keep failing."

We conducted a sub-study of more than eight thousand mature American believers—men and women who collectively spent 84 million days (more than a quarter century, on average) following Christ. About five in eight (63.1 percent) were women; the mean average age was forty-nine. (A third of the participants were between fifty and fifty-nine.)

Why this group? Mainly because of their wisdom and experience. Also, most mature Christians tap in to resources that help them grow spiritually. Many have consistent devotional lives—daily worship, prayer, and Bible reading. They're involved with discipleship and accountability groups; they're connected to thriving church communities. They share a desire to serve Christ and have embraced His call to evangelism.

Even so, these folks have something in common with young Christians and nonbelievers alike: *sin.*

SPIRITUAL ACTIVITIES AND DISCIPLINES

What do they know about overcoming sin that each of us should know?

Are there hot-button temptations that trip them up the most? If so, how often do they struggle with these?

What are the effects of temptation on spiritual growth?

Are men and women tempted in different ways?

What works in the fight against falling when tempted?

How does giving in to temptation affect Bible engagement?

The answers to these and other questions provide a detailed look at sin's effects *and* practical solutions all of us can apply. Let's move in for a closer look at issues related to the most frequent temptations of mature Christians.

Most Frequent Temptations for Women

- Gossip (12.3 percent)
- Overeating (12.1 percent)
- Spending Money (7.2 percent)

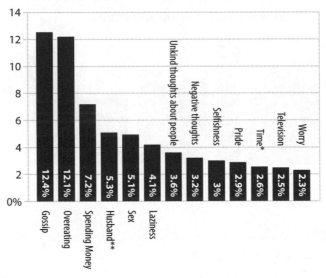

MOST FREQUENT TEMPTATIONS FOR WOMEN

* For the women we surveyed, *time* as a temptation refers to not using it wisely. In other words, idleness, laziness, spending time on hobbies instead of on responsibilities.

** For the women we surveyed, *husband* as a temptation refers to not fulfilling what they view as God's expectation for how a wife is supposed to love her husband. Some expressed anger toward their spouses and admitted that they are "often critical toward their husbands."

Most Frequent Temptations for Men

- Related to Wrong Choices About Sex (37.6 percent)
- Laziness (3.6 percent)
- Pride (3.5 percent)

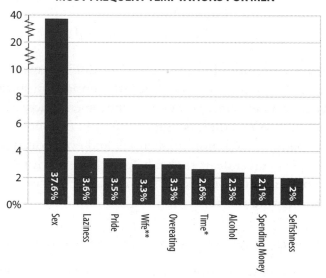

MOST FREQUENT TEMPTATIONS FOR MEN

* For the men we surveyed, *time* as a temptation refers to not using it wisely—exactly what women told us.

** For the men we surveyed, *wife* as a temptation refers to not fulfilling what they view as God's expectation for how a husband is supposed to love his wife. Here's how some men explained it: "the way I serve my wife," "being angry with my wife," "negative thoughts about my wife."

In a given day, women are tempted less often than men. As you can see from the graphs, temptation-types to which women are susceptible are more individually unique; among men, issues related to sexuality are by far the most common temptation source.[10]

How many times a day mature Christians are tempted to do something wrong: "fairly frequently."

- Tempted one to ten times daily: 80.8 percent
- Tempted at least three times daily: 49.9 percent
- Number of days per year Christians spent dwelling on temptations:

    Men: 342 (almost 94 percent of days)

    Women: 310 (almost 85 percent of days)

Infrequent temptations, in themselves, don't seem to "take root," and appear to have little negative impact on spiritual growth and daily living. However, as enticements increase and surface more often, there is proportionate likelihood of their becoming more and more influential, and even consuming, as they push out endeavors that help us thrive spiritually. It's commonsense stuff, yet people (even mature believers) aren't widely realizing this reality.

A majority says they fail at least some of the time.

- Give in to temptation "sometimes": 63.4 percent (almost two-thirds)[11]
- Give in to temptation "nearly all of the time": 15.9 percent

The experience of being tempted can have a straining or draining impact even if we don't capitulate. Further, many longtime believers (48.8 percent) hold that thinking about temptation is as sinful as acting out the enticement.[12] (An additional 9.6 percent said they're unsure whether this is true.)

Again, we are demonstrating throughout this book that engaging the Bible is the best means by which to resist temptation. Some mature Christ-followers admit a tendency to run from God and His Word in times of struggle—especially *after* they've given in to temptation. When we asked responders what keeps them from engaging Scripture, they (all responders) had almost total unawareness of the role temptation plays in their spiritual lives. Out of 8,285, only *twelve* listed temptation as a hindrance. And get this: Some said that while investing in the Bible has instilled in them a greater sensitivity to sin, it *also* has brought a slight increase in the frequency of feeling tempted.[13]

At first we were puzzled, even slightly shocked, as we analyzed. We then explored the relationship between the number of days per week believers were engaged in Scripture and the amount[14] of temptation they faced. Here's what we found: Those who consistently read or listened to the Bible (four-plus days a week) reported being tempted to engage in sinful behaviors *more often* during the typical day![15] Those engaged in Scripture one to three days weekly[16] or not at all[17] said they noticed slightly fewer enticements.

As we dug a bit deeper, the bigger picture began to emerge. This trend's counterintuitive direction had a simple explanation: Those actively invested and involved in God's Word had developed greater sensitivity to temptation and sin. In other words, they're more likely to perceive, remember, and report possible temptations because the standard of God's holy and righteous character is at the forefront of their consciousness.

With regard to temptation's long-term impacts, the following graph shows that more Scripture engagement is significantly associated with less time spent thinking about the desire to sin. Christ-followers who engaged the Bible at least four days a week spent an average of 318 days wrestling with a given difficult temptation. Those who spent little or no time in the Bible reported thinking about a particular temptation for an average of 384 days—more than two months longer.[18]

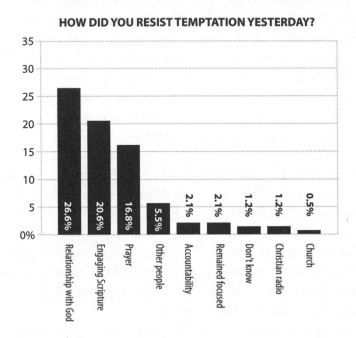

HOW DID YOU RESIST TEMPTATION YESTERDAY?

- Relationship with God: 26.6%
- Engaging Scripture: 20.6%
- Prayer: 16.8%
- Other people: 5.5%
- Accountability: 2.1%
- Remained focused: 2.1%
- Don't know: 1.2%
- Christian radio: 1.2%
- Church: 0.5%

What This Means for the "Stuck" Crowd

The bottom line: Even if we think or feel otherwise, we're not alone in our struggles. Once more, this is the answer to getting unstuck: *a thriving, two-way relationship with Jesus Christ founded on daily Bible engagement and time spent in prayer.*

Why, then, do so many of us flee from God and His Word when temptation strikes? Think about this: We surveyed believers who'd followed Christ ten or more years—many are older, wiser Bible readers who pray daily and are active in their churches. Yet they've all struggled with temptation, and for some the destructive behaviors following their failure to withstand have been seriously damaging: addictions to pornography, alcohol, drugs, gambling, compulsive lying and stealing, gossip, cheating, out-of-control anger and rage, violent thoughts . . . the list goes on and on.[19]

Does knowing that every one of them has battled and sometimes failed give you any sense of relief? If you're anything like me: yes *and* no. On the one hand, I'm relieved to be reassured that there's hope for everyone. On the other hand, I'm not only a little confused, I'm also seriously concerned.

Isn't a Christ-follower's life supposed to be *different*? Personally, over time, I've observed that replacement of a negative behavior with a positive one is a fairly reliable measurement of change in a person's life. Doesn't this apply to our faith as well? Well, here's what the Bible says:

The Holy Spirit enables us to overcome temptation.

Live by the Spirit, and you will not gratify the desires of the sinful nature. For the sinful nature desires what is contrary to the Spirit, and the Spirit what is contrary to the sinful nature. They are in conflict with each other, so that you do not do what you want. But if you are led by the Spirit, you are not under law.[20]

Trust in Christ as Lord and Savior; receive a new nature.

If anyone is in Christ, the new creation has come: The old has gone, the new is here![21]

Believers are called to live a holy life.

Since we have these promises, dear friends, let us purify ourselves from everything that contaminates body and spirit, perfecting holiness out of reverence for God.[22]

When I examine my actions, I quickly realize and admit I fight a win/lose battle with temptation. I strive to live by the Spirit, but sin and self win sometimes. I'm no stranger to the torment Larry Crabb describes:

> It's as if I'm innocently floating along in the freshwater stream of a good Christian life, doing nothing visibly or consciously wrong; and then without warning I find myself hurtling down a fast-moving river of delicious temptation, heading straight for the falls of misery. I feel no power to reverse direction, no will strong enough to paddle over to my nice Christian way of doing things. And worse, *at the moment I don't want to.* Flying over the falls seems more exciting than dangerous, more necessary than wrong. The thrill blinds me to the risk. And whatever love is within me dries up. I don't care about anyone or anything else, including you. The only sense I have as I think about you is a guilty anger.
>
> Standing in your grace seems more resistible than falling into my selfishness. It feels as if a compulsive force within me takes over my mind with lies, my heart with self-serving affections, and my will with unrelenting strength. Yielding becomes inevitable. And—I hate to admit this—part of me yields gladly with a smug sense of freedom. Father, what's happening to me?[23]

When I find myself thinking this way, my mind flashes to Henry Blackaby's difficult but nonnegotiable warning: "Master the sin at the door of your life before it brings its inevitable and disastrous consequences."

As a fellow temptation-fighting struggler, I empathize on many levels with Gene, whose tragic story we heard earlier. Can you relate to the heaping shame that can blanket the soul after giving in to sin? Can you relate to the searing agony of repeated failure? Can you relate to the numbing hopelessness of starting to think or even believe you can never change?

Yes, everyone is born a sinner, and temptation entices us all. But how do we obtain wisdom and strength to break lethal grips and gain the upper hand?

Yes, the Bible has the keys. But how do we live them out?

Yes, Christ is *the* answer. But what does this mean *practically*?

In the next chapter we'll respond to these questions. First, we'll look at how the enemy seeks to defeat us in temptation battles by using traps like shame, discouragement, and bitterness to veil God's truth. Next, we'll sort through confusion over what it means to grow spiritually. Then we'll look at how other believers are plotting a course toward real, transforming change.

Research Reveals: Four out of five respondents reported being tempted between one and ten times a day.

Encouraging Nudge: We're not alone in our battle with temptation, and win or lose, the results aren't confined to us either. Understanding the destructive forces lined up against us is the first step toward overcoming sin and avoiding its disastrous consequences. The second is learning to take our eyes off ourselves and consider how sin affects others. Caring for the souls of those we love is a higher aim than holding tightly to the fear of failing.

Take a look at unstuck.gotandem.com for more practical ways to grow spiritually. Do this every day during your forty-five-day journey.

Spiritual
Stepping Stones

● DAY 10

Scripture to Remember: Psalm 94:16–19

Question to Consider: When my foot is slipping—and temptation is overwhelming me—do I immediately turn to Jesus?

● DAY 11

Scripture to Remember: Genesis 3:1–24

Question to Consider: Is anything blocking my relationship with the Lord? (Are there sins I need to confess?)

● DAY 12

Scripture to Remember: James 1:13–15

Question to Consider: Which enticements are the most difficult for me to resist? How should I fight them?

five

Breakthroughs for the Broken

Only at the point where the insufficiency of natural strength is faced, felt, and admitted does divine empowering begin.[1]

—J. I. Packer

I blew it again.

I promised I wouldn't, but I did.

Later, my conscience unnerves me, and in frustration I writhe like a prisoner who squirms in his shackles but only wearies himself. Then I convince myself next time will be different. I blew it today, but I'll be strong tomorrow.

Yet tomorrow isn't different, and I begin to feel trapped.

How can I call myself a Christ-follower? I wonder. I'm a lousy follower, and my faith isn't really moving at all. The last thing I want to do is face God or read the Bible. Will He continue to accept me even though I mess up . . . over and over again?

Deep inside, I'd give anything to unload my secrets, but the fear of rejection keeps me silent.

So I remain isolated and miserable, suffocating behind a mask.

When I (Mike) first became a Christ-follower, I had this notion that I could conquer sin. Not just fighting it, resisting its grip—we all can and must do that. I mean overcome it to the point of living sin-free. I was well aware of my past sins (there've been many through the years), but I was convinced my future could be not merely different but completely different: *Try harder, read my Bible more, pray more, change some behaviors . . . and I can avoid all sin.*

The problem was, I kept blowing it.

Someday we'll be sinless, and then we'll never sin again—oh, how I long for that day. I so look forward to when we're selfless, a time when none of us will curse, kill, envy, lie, cheat, or steal. All of us who've committed our lives to Christ will be perfect when we stand before Him. On that day, "we shall be like him, for we shall see him as he is."[2]

Meanwhile, though, despite my zeal to please God, three equations had begun to rule my life, and not one of them was adding up:

Legalism + Works = Christianity
Good Behavior + Performance = Forgiveness
Rules + Self-Control = Faith

Before long I got a sour taste of reality. Living this way sets us up for loads of disappointment and shame. No matter how many rules I followed and how well I seemed to perform, I was still plagued by the tendency to sin. A minister once explained how he sought to ward off temptation:

I ask the Holy Spirit to strengthen me to resist sin and to remind me of God's holiness and will for my life. And then I recite verses like 1 Corinthians 10:12–13. As I ponder the Lord's overwhelming generosity and goodness, I know that my response must be the total dedication of my life to Him.

He went on to cite one of his favorite spiritual-growth books, reminding me of what happens when we mess up: "God removes our guilt, provides forgiveness, implants in us a positive life-principle of goodness and meaning, restores fruitfulness, and reconciles us to Himself and to our fellowmen."[3]

I certainly couldn't argue—he was right. I then realized, though, that believing these truths and acting on them were two different things. While my heart was committed to Christ, and I knew my sins were forgiven, my feet were still planted here on earth, walking moment by moment in a fallen and broken world. My struggles and problems wouldn't let go easily; for sure they wouldn't vanish merely on the basis of my belief in the truth of God's Word.

When eventually I turned my attention to the apostle Paul's story, I was struck by the frustration and agony he experienced as he struggled:

> I do not understand what I do. For what I want to do I do not do, but what I hate I do. . . . For I have the desire to do what is good, but I cannot carry it out. For I do not do the good I want to do, but the evil I do not want to do—this I keep on doing. Now if I do what I do not want to do, it is no longer I who do it, but it is sin living in me that does it.[4]

Even Paul, who was personally called and commissioned by Jesus Christ, wrestled with temptation and struggled with sin. I like how *The Message* renders his thoughts and expressions during intense adversity:

So I wouldn't get a big head, I was given the gift of a handicap to keep me in constant touch with my limitations. Satan's angel did his best to get me down; what he in fact did was push me to my knees. No danger then of walking around high and mighty! At first I didn't think of it as a gift, and begged God to remove it. Three times I did that, and then he told me,

My grace is enough; it's all you need.

My strength comes into its own in your weakness.[5]

Once I heard this I was glad to let it happen. I quit focusing on the handicap and began appreciating the gift. Gradually, increasingly empowered with Christ's great might, I can take limitations in stride and with good cheer. When shortcomings and shortfalls cut me down to size—and when I face opposition, abuse, accidents, bad breaks—I take my eyes off me and look to Him. I let go and let Him take over. The weaker I get, the stronger I become.

Getting Unstuck: Paul's Math

Paul[6] recognized something I'd missed: He *hadn't* and *would never* attain perfection in this lifetime. He accepted that he wouldn't become complete and mature this side of heaven.[7] He embraced a realistic view of himself—which meant acknowledging he was human and had an innate sin tendency.[8]

Yes, Christ's life-changing power was alive in his heart, and yes, His sacrifice on the cross delivers from sin and death. But Paul also knew that believers don't become divine automatons when we receive salvation by faith (i.e., when we're justified). He knew that he, like every Christian, would experience a process of being shaped into Christ's likeness (i.e., as we're sanctified). And he knew that the completion, the finality of deliverance from sin and triumph over spiritual death, will come after this earthly life (i.e., when we're glorified). So Paul knew where he needed to be in the meantime: on his knees, experiencing God's grace.

The apostle had a healthy grasp of three "equations" that *do* add up:

Christ + Salvation = Christianity
Love + Grace = Forgiveness
Surrender + Freedom = Faith

To me, the message was clear: God denounced my sin and, like Paul, I needed to change. Still, in seeking to follow Christ, I had to remind myself I might fall on my face along the way. The solution is to keep getting back up, to continue submitting to God, to persist in surrendering to growth.

One thing I do: Forgetting what is behind and straining toward what is ahead, I press on toward the goal to win the prize for which God has called me heavenward in Christ Jesus.[9]

Pursue obedience.

While maintaining an accurate view of his humanity, Paul made it his goal to live a changed life. Our research backs up the success (though not ease) of his "obedience principle." Christ-followers can recover from sin and overcome self-defeating behaviors—and ultimately get unstuck spiritually—if we learn how to "crawl, walk, and run" when we face a battle. (We respond differently depending on the struggle and on the season of our faith. Sometimes we behave maturely and steadfastly walk or even run; at other moments we respond like a new believer and just crawl.)

Maintain focus.

When he failed, Paul didn't despair in his sin. He embraced Christ's forgiveness through confession and repentance, and he got back into the race. You may stumble when you're on the move, but you'll reach the finish line if you get back up and keep going forward.

Leave the past in the past.

Having received God's forgiveness for past sins, Paul let them go. That freed all his resources to follow (love and obey) Christ.

Relinquish any fantasy of control.

At times we get caught up in the illusion that we rule our lives and determine our steps. When life is smooth, we feel pretty good about ourselves . . . but then the rug is pulled out underneath and we're devastated. Paul knew this all too well, so instead of placing confidence in his ability to avoid failure, he placed faith in the certainty that even if he missed the mark or fell short, Jesus wouldn't. "Therefore I will boast all the more gladly about my weaknesses, so that Christ's power may rest on me."[10]

"The Power Pitfall" and "The Power Principle"

Here's an important distinction: We *will* wrestle with sin in this life, and we won't experience its complete vanquishing until we meet the Lord in heaven. *However*—and this is important—because of what Jesus has accomplished for us, we now are no longer slaves to sin.

> Do not offer the parts of your body to sin, as instruments of wickedness, but rather offer yourselves to God, as those who have been brought from death to life; and offer the parts of your body to him as instruments of righteousness. For sin

shall not be your master, because you are not under law, but under grace.[11]

We have a new identity in Christ, so we have a choice to make: Yield to our old nature . . . or to our new one. It's at these moments during our life race that things can turn ugly. We trip, fail, and fall. Some of us get so discouraged we don't bother getting back up—or taking another step—and our spiritual growth comes to a halt.

But we needn't give in to hopelessness! Instead, we must continually "put off" or "put away" the old characteristics and "put on" traits of our new life.[12] Erwin Lutzer reminds us that doing so means building into our lives qualities that up until now we may have avoided or rejected:

> There are many ways to fail in the Christian life. But all of them begin with lack of discipline, a conscious decision to take the easy route. Paul says, "I discipline my body and bring it under control." The lie is that the body cannot be disciplined, for indeed it can, especially with the help of the Holy Spirit, who gives us self-control.[13]

J. I. Packer says it well:

> The secret to discipline is divine empowerment, which builds internal strength. Fortunately for us, the key to God's strength is our own weakness. Through humble dependence on Jesus Christ we find the strength to put off our old life and to grow in our new one. The power pitfall is self-reliance and failure to see that without Christ we can do nothing that is spiritually significant. The power principle is that divine strength is perfected in human weakness.
>
> If I could remember each day of my life that the way to grow stronger is to grow weaker, if I would accept that each day's frustrations, obstacles, and accidents are God's ways

of making me acknowledge my weakness so that growing stronger might become a possibility for me, if I did not betray myself into relying on myself—my knowledge, my expertise, my position, my skill with words, and so on—what a difference it would make to me![14]

The Enemy Seeks to "Veil" the Truth

Even though sin is not our master because the Holy Spirit's power is on our side, Paul also knew that another force is at work on us, seeking to destroy our relationship with Christ, distort the truth, and block spiritual growth. I'm talking, of course, about the workings of Satan.

His very name means *adversary,* and despite what some say, God's Word does not portray him as a metaphor or a symbol of evil. Satan, a created being, rebelled against God. He is very real, very dangerous, and very active in the world today, enticing people toward evil.

God calls him an inciter,[15] an accuser,[16] a sinner,[17] a murderer, and a liar.[18] The devil is pure evil—he and his troops (other created beings who rebelled with him) are viciously attacking God's kingdom. His target: our souls.

Charles Stanley warns:

> He can and will attempt to drag you down into such deep bondage that you will lose your joy in living. Some may call this bondage oppression, depression, or addiction. If the devil can pull you into bondage, you will have no peace, no zest for living, and perhaps even no will to continue living.[19]

He adds, "The devil will do his utmost to completely destroy anything that is essential for abundant life."[20] Like others have before him, Gene[21] wrestled with unmet desires, unsatisfied drives, unrealized dreams, and an unfulfilled destiny.[22]

And the enemy's number-one goal is to separate us from the source of life—Jesus Christ—through at least three tactics: (1) a strained relationship with our Savior, (2) a clouded mind, and (3) a hardened heart. Once again: Accept a bit of compromise here, a seemingly tiny shortcut there, and little by little, before we realize it, the patterns become set. That's why a simple lesson I've learned will keep ringing true: *If you aren't caught up in a sin, don't mess with it; if you are or think you are, get help.*

Pulling Back the Veil

Paul added another item to the mix, one that's most encouraging for all who feel stuck and defeated by the enemy:

> *Relationship (with Christ) + Truth (in the Word) = Spiritual Growth*

While the enemy strives to veil our eyes, he's no more than an annoying mosquito compared to the power of God. The Bible gives us clues about his limitations, such as when God said, " 'Everything he [Job] has is in your power, but on the man himself do not lay a finger.' Then Satan went out from the presence of the Lord."[23] The devil operates on a leash; God holds it.

The author of Hebrews assures us that Christ rendered powerless the influence of fear Satan held over humanity: "Since the children have flesh and blood, he too shared in their humanity so that by his death he might break the power of him who holds the power of death—that is, the devil."[24]

Satan *wants* us to believe he still holds that power (and unlimited others). However, as a created being, he isn't sovereign or all-powerful, and he's not God's equal opposite. The

gospel revealed by Jesus Christ and His apostles excludes and rejects any dualism wherein two equivocal powers struggle for control. Many Christians live as though Satan were as mighty as God; nothing could be further from the truth! He ultimately stands no chance.[25]

Through Jesus, because of what He has accomplished on our behalf, the veil can be pulled back from our human eyes, and we can know truth. C. S. Lewis explained the beginning point of our hope this way:

> Christianity tells people to repent and promises them for-giveness. It therefore has nothing (as far as I know) to say to people who do not know that they have anything to repent of and who do not feel that they need forgiveness. It is after you have realized that there is a real Moral Law, and a Power behind that law, and that you have broken that law and put yourself wrong with that Power—it is after all this, and not a moment sooner, that Christianity begins to talk.[26]

The Meaning of "Maturity"

We've explored some of the elements that cause us to stall spiritually—stuff that keeps us trapped, tired, weary, and otherwise immobilized. We've seen the importance of developing a humble, daily dependence on Christ. Now it's time to look at how to get our faith growing again.

What does it mean, exactly, to *grow spiritually*?

We could consult a dictionary, open a guide to theological terms, or spend some time sifting comments we find through a search engine. Chances are we'd find so many variations that we'd end up even more confused.

Recent studies suggest that many Christians, even pastors, have difficulty defining *spiritual growth* and *spiritual maturity*. It's not surprising, then, that answers among adults from different faith backgrounds are wildly diverse. We found the most common responses provided only a vague definition, such as:

- "to know what you do or say"
- "you grow with God"
- "to be mature in thoughts, words, and deeds"
- "experience with God"
- "strong faith"

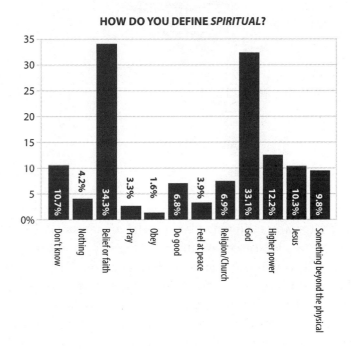

HOW DO YOU DEFINE *SPIRITUAL*?

The next most common responses described *spiritual maturity* as being firm in one's spiritual beliefs. For example:

- "knowing what you believe in spiritually, not something you can see, but believe in it anyhow"

- "really believe in, and understand, your beliefs"
- "having a full understanding of the religion, being able to connect and integrate it into your life and knowing right from wrong"
- "to be unwavering in your fidelity to your religion"

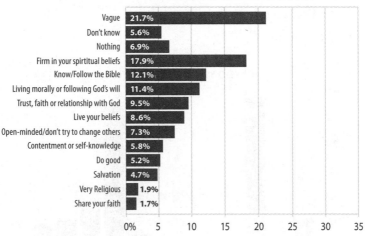

DEFINITIONS OF SPIRITUAL MATURITY

Category	Percentage
Vague	21.7%
Don't know	5.6%
Nothing	6.9%
Firm in your spirtitual beliefs	17.9%
Know/Follow the Bible	12.1%
Living morally or following God's will	11.4%
Trust, faith or relationship with God	9.5%
Live your beliefs	8.6%
Open-minded/don't try to change others	7.3%
Contentment or self-knowledge	5.8%
Do good	5.2%
Salvation	4.7%
Very Religious	1.9%
Share your faith	1.7%

As salvation is life's single most important element, placing our faith in and following Christ is the most crucial decision we'll ever make. Living in and growing in Christ thereafter is the daily pursuit of a forgiven life. His grace is free; as we acknowledge our brokenness, we allow Him to work in our hearts on all levels. He moves into our hurts, hopes, resentments, desires, mistakes—each and every last "region" of us. He alone truly knows our most private thoughts, longings, and struggles.

Isn't it awe-inspiring that He (and only He) can deliver us?

Even so, it's no wonder we have such difficulty defining spiritual growth and maturity. With all the possible baggage combinations we carry around, each personal journey will be specific to the one who undertakes it. For every one of us, this transformational process (more formally known as *sanctification*) is vitally, inherently part of living out our salvation.[27]

While the initial acceptance of salvation (more formally known as *justification*) is absolutely necessary, it's also just the beginning of living a free life. We rarely know what we're getting into when we ask Christ to examine our hearts and deliver us from our own weaknesses, but we cannot become people growing in holiness without it.

This is exactly what a young believer named Kelly discovered early in her walk with God.

Getting Unstuck Means Digging Deep

Kelly's childhood was badly marred. Her father and mother abused alcohol—and her. Dark closets. Frequent nightmares. Awful secrets.

Her teenage years brought more of the same, yet no one knew—nobody saw through the fancy mirage. Both parents were professionals, prestigious and highly respected in the community. Kelly had expensive clothes and her own car. Everyone thought they were a model family.

When it came time for college, Kelly chose a school several states away and came to feel as if she'd finally escaped. No one sent care packages or "We miss you" cards, but that was okay; she didn't wish to hear from "back there." She spent weekends on campus, spent winter and spring breaks at roommates' homes. She imagined what it would be like to have a loving family.

One day in the library, Kelly met Jeff.[28] Within hours they were planning a first date. Two weeks later they considered themselves a couple. Throughout the next semester, everything Kelly had ever known changed dramatically. Suddenly someone loved her, believed in her, and treated her like a queen.

Jeff knew God and talked openly with Him on a regular basis. He began praying about Kelly, and soon she had a desire to know the Lord too.

They started attending a fellowship together and became a part of a cell group. Kelly had never known such love or heard such encouragement and hope. The Word of God was beautiful; she especially liked the Psalms. Yet building trust and nurturing relationships was difficult. She harbored resentment and hatred over her past—and for the pain her family had caused.

Then one night in a Bible study, it happened.

She wanted to receive salvation. She longed to know God as her Father. She realized Jesus had died for her. She desired everything her group family had talked about: forgiveness, love, life everlasting.

If the purpose of her life had been to bring her into this moment in time, Kelly felt it was worth what she'd endured. She prayed; she wept tears of repentance. Jesus was now real to her. She felt the Father's love pouring down upon her. The group wrapped arms of love around her and praised God for the miracle in her life.

Five years later the happily married Kelly had grown much in God's knowledge and grace. However, even though she and Jeff had a supportive fellowship family, her relationship with her parents still was completely broken. Basically, she was doing her best not to think about her past.

In the following months, Jeff and Kelly became avid hikers. During one trek on property Jeff had inherited, they discovered such a wondrous piece of paradise in the woods that they began making plans to build a log cabin there.

It was spectacular. Sunsets blazed magenta and scarlet. Deer fed in the valley below. West Virginia's misty-blue mountains rolled across the horizon.

Thereafter they drew sketches and discussed how they could build the place themselves. They hiked back to the site, hammered wooden stakes into the ground, and attached string to form the structure's layout. They planned an expansive front porch that faced the mountainous overlook.

Anxious to get started, they broke ground, slinging shovels of dirt into a wheelbarrow. But they quickly encountered a problem. Jeff hit something that just wouldn't budge.

Precisely where the foundation footers were to be dug, a root of massive proportions was beneath the surface. Swinging the mattock as hard as he could and striking with all his might, Jeff couldn't even chip the root—it seemed petrified. He attacked it from every angle and discovered a conjoined network of smaller roots, intertwined and gnarled together to make the ground virtually rock solid.

As Kelly sat down and watched her husband battle the root, a wave of emotion overtook her. Then, frustrated, she got up and walked away. She didn't even want to consider giving up their plans for this spot. On cliffs high above the valley, she pulled out a pocket Bible and began to read.

Quietly, God spoke: *"The root is deep, and it has become hard like stone. Even though it is deep and seems impossible to remove, it isn't. You can't remove it alone, but I will remove it for you if you will allow Me to."*

It was a moment she would never forget. She felt the awe of her Father God speaking intimately to her. And she knew He wasn't talking about the physical root; He meant the petrified root in her heart. She'd tried to keep the hate and unforgiveness hidden below the surface, but now she wanted it gone—completely out of her life.

On that ridge, God's love was melting her, and tears began to fall. She squeezed her eyes shut and continued: "I can't deal with this any longer, Lord. Remove this lifelong root of pain and bitterness. Take it from me and in its place give me love and forgiveness. Heal me from my past. Let me love the family who hurt me. Allow them to see your love living in me, and save them, in Jesus' name."

What We Can Do to Grow

When Kelly took that crucial step, a tremendous weight was lifted from her.

God began a transformational process: He took her to the very place that had brought about her being spiritually stuck, and He released her to grow.

He asked a few things of Kelly:

a step of obedience
a focus fixed on growth
leaving the past in the past
a desire to surrender all to Christ—past, present, and future

Most of all, He wanted her desire: "Love the Lord your God with all your heart and with all your soul and with all your mind and with all your strength."[29]

Does God have *your* desire?

Are you ready to take the first gutsy steps toward spiritual growth?

Christ wants us to know Him. He doesn't play games—He gave His own life for us, and He is God's very own Word!

106

Spiritual maturity, defined: It's knowing and living the principles in Scripture—God's Word to us.

Here's a bit of guidance regarding *focus* and *desire:* Don't let yourself fall victim to distraction. Don't try to define Scripture without being immersed in it. And don't rely on expert advice—read it and find out for yourself.

Don't burn out; keep yourselves fueled and aflame. Be alert servants of the Master, cheerfully expectant. Don't quit in hard times; pray all the harder. Help needy Christians; be inventive in hospitality.[30]

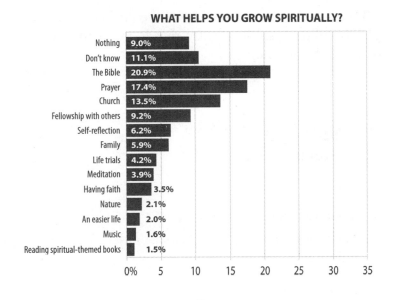

WHAT HELPS YOU GROW SPIRITUALLY?

Nothing	9.0%
Don't know	11.1%
The Bible	20.9%
Prayer	17.4%
Church	13.5%
Fellowship with others	9.2%
Self-reflection	6.2%
Family	5.9%
Life trials	4.2%
Meditation	3.9%
Having faith	3.5%
Nature	2.1%
An easier life	2.0%
Music	1.6%
Reading spiritual-themed books	1.5%

0% 5 10 15 20 25 30 35

In Part Two, "The Powered by Four Solution," we'll explore how spiritual growth begins when we engage God's Word, enter a two-way conversation with Him, and move from notional belief to being a relational Christ-follower.

Research Reveals: We can recover from self-defeating choices—and, ultimately, get unstuck spiritually—if we learn how to "crawl, walk, and run" when we face a battle.

Encouraging Nudge: The way to fix a mixed-up and sin-filled heart is through meaningful connection with God. That relationship goes far beyond a quick "quiet time"; it's about finding the joy of a life surrendered to Christ, one that understands the power of obedience without terror of failure. We grow spiritually by realizing, then resembling the character of our forgiving heavenly Father.

Take a look at unstuck.gotandem.com for more practical ways to grow spiritually. Do this every day during your forty-five-day journey.

Spiritual
Stepping Stones

● **DAY 13**

Scripture to Remember: Malachi 4:1–3
Question to Consider: What healing touch do I need from the Lord?

● **DAY 14**

Scripture to Remember: Deuteronomy 4:32–40
Question to Consider: Do I live as though God truly is all-powerful and all-loving?

DAY 15

Scripture to Remember: Matthew 15:21–28

Question to Consider: Do I live as though Jesus loves me fully, no matter my hang-ups and imperfections?

Part Two

The Powered by
Four Solution

By the End of Part Two You'll Be Able to:

- Move your faith from notional belief to a relational life
- Engage the Bible (rather than only read it)
- Receive, reflect on, and respond to God's personal message for you
- Apply the Powered by Four Solution to nurture your spiritual growth

six

Radically Relational (Not Too Religious)

The goal is not that you should become a great Bible scholar. It's not about mere intellectual assent to a set of doctrines. The goal is that you should be like Jesus—and the Scriptures can help you with that. I don't need to read the Bible because I'm a great saint. I read the Bible because I'll find God there. It's about a daily walk with this person Jesus.[1]

—Rich Mullins

Theresa was practically raised in church. Her hardworking, country-folk parents had come from a culture of stern fundamentalism: Women wore long skirts and long hair; the preacher sermonized loud and long; the Sunday school classes emphasized long lists of rules for acquiring personal holiness.

Theresa was taught that if she toed the line, doing the do's and not doing the don'ts, then she'd attain the fullness of Christ.

That is, her behavior would make her either acceptable or unacceptable to God.

As she grew, she did her best to "always be a good girl" and was very proud of being a good *Christian* too. She knew the Scriptures inside and out and had all the right answers during Bible studies. She stayed in step with church elders, which scored her major brownie points with the higher-ups. Among her peers she was the "Super Saint with the big, bright future."

God must like me very, very much, she convinced herself.

Theresa thought she had Him in her back pocket—she'd figured out the entire Christian life by age fifteen.

A few years down the road, though, she had an anxious pang: *Something isn't adding up.*

And then a second: *Something's missing.*

She was well into her college years when anxious pangs turned into nagging thoughts she couldn't dismiss: *I've been living the right way; why can't I sense God's presence in my life anymore? Where did He go?*

She felt completely alone, separated from God despite all her zeal.

Now Theresa would pull out her journal and flip open her Bible only to find reading the Scriptures a chore. God's Word felt intermittently lifeless, impractical, irrelevant. Her prayer life also had lost its passion. In fact, her whole faith increasingly seemed rigid and mechanical.

One particular evening—during a moment she'll never forget—an unthinkable fear flashed through her head: *Maybe I've lost Jesus.*

Night after night thereafter she sat in her apartment, feeling utterly cut off from her Lord and Savior, convinced that He'd left her.

She cried out to Him, yet He seemed silent.

What had happened?

The "good Christian kid" had grown into a smart young woman whose big, bright future actually was more promising than ever. So why did God seem absent? Why couldn't she hear Him speaking?

Theresa's own words tell the story.

Losing the "God of Rules"

After years of trying to be "the model Christian," God was gone. What now? How can I resuscitate a spiritual heart that isn't beating?

One day in college I spent time in reflection, examining my life, yet the Lord seemed nowhere near. I searched and searched, I prayed and prayed. But my heart's deep coolness and emptiness remained. It wasn't just that I couldn't feel God. I soon realized I couldn't really feel anything. I didn't laugh or cry or feel sad or happy. I just was—and I felt very alone.

For weeks and months I cried out to God to come back. I did everything I could to get His attention. While I'd spent most of my life avoiding countless don'ts, now I was carrying out nearly all the do's. I went to church as often as possible, even sang in the choir. I hung out with godly men and women.

But all the while my heart felt dead and very much afraid. I couldn't stop thinking that the "tried and tested" formulas I was raised on were missing the mark. It's not about reining me in or conforming to someone else's idea of what a "good Christian" is. Something's missing. Something much bigger . . . and much, much better.

Yet why the silence? What had I done to deserve abandonment?

Then one balmy Florida night—I lived in Jacksonville at the time—a song caught me by surprise. I was bent over the sink, washing dishes in my little apartment, as music blasted through my radio: The words caught my attention because they spoke of seeking God in the dark, when the only way to find Him would be to soften your heart.

Those convicting words pierced my heart.

It suddenly made sense. I instantly realized I'd been searching for the "God of Rules"—a god whose love and favor depended on something He required—no, demanded—in return. In all honesty, I was looking for a god who doesn't exist. I was searching in the dark.

With tears dripping into the dishwater I cried out, "Show me how to love you! Show me how to soften my heart toward you. Show me how to know you . . . and hear you. Change me!" I wept and wept as four years of numbness began to melt away.

In the weeks that followed I began to experience a closer relationship with Jesus. What changed for me? I gradually came to understand the secret that would guide my relationship with God for the rest of my life: I need to fall in love with Jesus!

I realized I need to pursue Christ as my closest companion and best friend. I must put all else aside to be with Him. He must be my heart's priority, even while I attend to life's everyday business.

Being in relationship with Him isn't about religion or following rules. To be in true relationship with Him I must pursue . . .

. . . His heart

. . . His passions

. . . His character

. . . the truth.

I must be His hands, His feet, a reflection of His love to others.

Nurturing a relationship involves trust, transparency, surrender, and above all a two-way connection. Close friends—especially lovers—must talk and grow together daily, not occasionally.

My conversations with God had been pretty one-sided. Usually I was moving my lips and doing most or all the talking . . . hardly any real listening, no shared communication. My head was full of Bible facts and knowledge—along with my notions of God's characteristics and priorities. I was fixed on "churchianity": looking Christian, saying Christian things, impressing Christian family and friends, and thinking all this also was impressing God.

My heart, on the other hand—it was, as I said, very empty, very numb.

Falling in Love With the God of the Bible

Jesus began a painful work in me.

It didn't happen overnight, and it came with a mix of joy, tears, and the heart-pounding expectation that my life was taking a radical new turn.

He slowly stripped away the masks, the false assumptions, the bad theology, the idols, and the chilly layers between Him and me. Little by little my heart warmed up to Him.

Somewhere along the way I rediscovered the amazing link between meditating on the Holy Scriptures and the intimate relationship with God I was seeking. Bible reading, reflection, and prayer helped me engage in the intimate conversation that actually flows through the sixty-six letters God has given us!

I pursued each activity in harmony, and His Word began to penetrate my heart at all levels. I began to hear Him speaking to me.

It became important that I practice each discipline in order to gain the fullness of His presence and His Word as He spoke to my spirit daily. It was a true growing process. It took time to learn to balance reading with meditating and reflecting (on God's Word, through journaling) and then "praying the Scriptures" to agree with what He already has said and promised!

At times God gave me a hug through His Word. He told me how much He loved me and talked about eternity with Him. At other moments His words really stung. He challenged me to deal with some rough places in my heart: bitterness to overcome, forgiveness to give, control to let go of.

Most of the time, His Word brought me to my knees in humility and worship. He revealed His everlasting strength, wisdom, and majesty. I was beginning to see that the ultimate use of the Scriptures is not merely for knowledge; God's Word also deepens our relationship with Jesus. After all, we're called to the Potter's wheel to be molded and shaped into His image. The Scriptures are the tools the Father uses to do His work. Submitting to the truth can soften a heart of stone and cause it to become a heart of clay.

This was a time to rethink what the Bible is and how I approach it.

As Ruth Haley Barton suggests in her excellent book *Sacred Rhythms*, it's important that Christ-followers long to hear a word from God that's personal and that takes us deeper into the connection our souls crave. "The study of Scripture is important," she affirms, "but if we stop there, we will eventually hit a wall spiritually. . . . Our soul knows that there must be something more."[2]

I was ready for more.

Hearing His Voice . . . at Last!

In order to hear Jesus and share a two-way connection, I had to slow down and engage the Bible. This meant receiving God's Word in both my mind and my heart. It meant savoring and reflecting on His story. It meant responding to what He would say to my own experiences; sometimes He prompted me to change a behavior, conform to His will, or face tough issues.

More than anything, though, it meant beginning to believe He loves and accepts me just as I am . . . and there's nothing I can do to make Him love me more than He already does. Once I got that, the joy of walking with Him became my strength and motivation for submitting to His life-changing Words. Our love relationship deepened because I didn't have to fear not measuring up and confronting the possibility of His rejecting me. His Word has taught me to trust in His character with no "shadow of turning."[3] I could change because I had the freedom to change—a freedom I received from being loved by Him. His Words set me free.

So I began the sacred pursuit of Jesus through the Scriptures and through intimate times of personal worship in God's presence . . . right in my bedroom or living room or kitchen! I set aside time to spend with Him—receiving His Word and tuning my spiritual ears to hear His voice.

I later moved to an early-American house that had a beautifully carved antique oak mantel over an old wrought-iron fireplace. Every day I'd come home from work, throw my stuff on the couch, and go stand before it to wait. Often my Bible was open before me. It was a symbolic gesture—I wanted the fire of His heart and His love inside me. This became my meeting place with God, and whether or not there was an actual fire roaring, my heart always burned for Him in that spot, and He always, always met me there.

Jesus would come and speak softly to my heart. He'd remind me of the day, show me my own heart, reveal myself to me and gently begin to heal and coax and teach—and love me into His image.

Looking back now it seems strange that even though I'd grown up like a young Bible scholar, conforming to its law and obeying its rules, I'd still missed its essential truth: I am called to a dynamic, life-giving intimacy with Jesus. He speaks to me; He leads me into deeper love and deeper truth and deeper life through His love letters written just for me (and just for you). It is only through relationship with Jesus that I can become intimately engaged with Him through His Word. And as I feed on His Word to me, I am changed.

Rich Mullins sang of the Bible that he did not make it; rather, it was making him. He declared it to be the truth and not man's invention.

Yes, it is making me . . . and remaking me.

Becoming Relational

Loving God with all our heart, soul, and mind[4]
Engaging the Bible in a two-way connection with Jesus
Pondering God's Word deep in our heart

These basics of faith should be second nature to every Christ-follower, right? Yet as Theresa observed, somewhere along the way we can risk settling for a "god of rules." She learned what we've seen: in this sense there are two types.

Notional Christ-followers believe in a concept of Christ and "interact" one-way with Him. A notional believer communicates in his or her mind to a *notion* of Christ in lieu of a two-way relationship with the true Lord and Savior. And, again, there are no significant behavioral differences between the notional believer and a person who claims not to follow Christ at all.

Relational Christ-followers have a two-way relationship with the actual Christ through saving faith based on God's Word. This begins when we come to grips with our sin, recognize our need for salvation, and receive Jesus Christ as our Savior. His Holy Spirit places us into His body (the community of faith, His church) and initiates a connection fostered consistently by prayer (talking with God) and engaging Scripture (hearing from God). Genuine faith produces measurable behavioral results reflected in choices and actions.

Theresa knew she had to give up her own notions about Jesus and begin pursuing the one true God. "Everyone seeks intimacy with God, whether or not they're willing to admit it," she says. "Ignore this need and you end up looking for Him in the wrong places. It's sort of like drinking the sand because you believe it's an oasis, but it's only a mirage."

God designed us to bond relationally with Him. As Doug Banister notes:

All of us are on a lifelong quest to know Him more intimately. We must learn how to bond with Him if we are to become the people He has called us to be. The cost of failing to bond with God can be staggering: addiction, low self-confidence, depression, religiosity, burnout, and relational problems.[5]

The God of the Bible is relational. The three members of the Trinity—God the Father, God the Son, and God the Holy Spirit—exist in relationship together. Jesus describes their relationship as intensely intimate, saying to the Father, "You are in me and I am in you."[6]

The creation story, Banister observes, is an account of a relational God creating a man and a woman He could bond with, revealing to us and through us the unity of the God-head. We find a clue about God's heart when He says, "Let us make mankind in our image, in our likeness."[7] God, who exists in relationship, creates people who bear this same relational likeness.[8]

God didn't form just one human being, but two. When Adam was still the only human, God said, "It is not good for the man to be alone."[9] *Why* isn't it—was relationship with God "not enough"? Evidently Adam needed to be in relationship with God *and* with other people. This is why Jesus sums up the Bible's teaching in two commands: Love God and love your neighbor.[10] *Relationship* is the essence of the gospel, the good news: the restoration of the relationship for which our Father originally created us.

Henry Cloud writes:

Relationship, or bonding, then, is at the foundation of God's nature. Since we are created in His likeness, relationship is our most fundamental need, the very foundation of who we are. Without relationship, without attachment to God and others, we can't be our true selves. We can't be truly human.[11]

"Lukewarm" Faith Isn't Really Faith at All

Considering the importance of a thriving relationship, which by nature develops over time, and understanding that religious rituals and practices can't save us, I (Arnie) have wrestled with difficult questions about sincere faith.

Are we mistaken and even misled in presuming people are saved who have not allowed their relationship with God to take hold and grow? What about someone who's never experienced meaningful changes in his or her life?

For example, what if I pray for salvation and say my heart belongs to Christ and yet I maintain a sexual relationship with a woman who's not my wife? If I've demonstrated no change—I don't pray (disdain relationship with God), ignore my Bible (don't want to hear God speak), avoid church (reject connection with Christ-followers), and am disinterested in or loathe to grow closer to Christ (perhaps my life is even the same as it was before) . . . *am I truly a Christian?*

Thankfully, God is the only and final judge. He knows whose faith is genuine. I can say that I've worked with some desperate people and have witnessed real victory over addiction and sin. Through it all, Paul's words once again ring loudly in my ears: "If anyone is in Christ, the new creation has come: The old has gone, the new is here!"[12]

Four other words scream through my brain, as well: *"I never knew you."*

These are horrible words to consider—maybe the most terrifying in the Bible. Jesus spoke them while teaching on a mountainside:

Not everyone who says to me, "Lord, Lord," will enter the kingdom of heaven, but only the one who does the will of my Father who is in heaven. Many will say to me on that day, "Lord, Lord, did we not prophesy in your name and in your name drive out demons and in your name perform many miracles?" Then I will tell them plainly, "I never knew you. Away from me, you evildoers!"[13]

I know Jesus was warning about religious phonies and people He'd just described as "ferocious wolves" in sheep's clothing.[14] *But what about the times when I doubt? What about the seasons when I don't feel close to God? What about the struggles I often battle?*

Is Jesus saying it's all about a perfect score? If I don't always do the do's and avoid the don'ts . . . is it possible I could miss eternity too?

The answer is *no*. God loves us passionately no matter our imperfections. Change does not bring about salvation— rather genuine salvation produces change in us as God patiently works it all out in us, with us, step-by-step.

Here's something that troubles me: Too often when believers exhibit no change in their lives or revert to former lifestyles, we refer to them as "unsanctified believers" or "carnal Christians" (or the like). Based on my research, not theology, the term *carnal Christian* appears to be useless with regard to discipleship and genuine faith.

From a scientific standpoint, if no behavior separates the "carnal Christian" from the non-Christian, there's no such thing as a carnal Christian.[15] Rather, that person made a profession of faith but remains (persists, still is rooted) in sinfulness. Again, only God can judge the heart. But where there's no changed behavior, there's reason to suspect there is no genuineness of salvation.[16]

Here's what Jesus said:

Do people pick grapes from thornbushes, or figs from thistles? Likewise, every good tree bears good fruit, but a bad tree bears bad fruit. . . . Thus, by their fruit you will recognize them.[17]

The test of true life in Christ is spiritual growth, not verbal profession.

There are significant behavioral and lifestyle differences between Christ-followers who know what the Bible is and what it's for and those who don't. *Engaging God's Word works!*

If you've been looking in darkness, are you ready to stop? Are you yearning to fall in love with Jesus and begin pursuing Him with all your heart?

As Theresa spent time with Him, pursuing His heart, she began to see, to experience, to know Him as her King and her Lord, her Protector and her Provider, and most of all, the Lover of her soul.

———◈———

It was rethinking how I (Mike) engage the Bible and how learning to connect with God through Scripture made the difference for me as well. In the next chapter I'll take you back to my spiritual breakthrough.

———◈———

Research Reveals: In order to get unstuck spiritually, we must begin to have a two-way relationship with Jesus Christ and endeavor to live as a relational Christ-follower.

Encouraging Nudge: Knowing God through experience differs profoundly from knowing *about* God from sermons, devotional guides, and secondhand accounts. God says we cannot say we know Him unless we experience Him in personal relationship. As with the relationships we share with other people, consistent Bible engagement and our related steps toward growing closer to God are about two-way connections: communication, listening, shared meaning, trust, and growing together.

Take a look at unstuck.gotandem.com for more practical ways to grow spiritually. Do this every day during your forty-five-day journey.

Spiritual
Stepping Stones

DAY 16

Scripture to Remember: Daniel 2:19–23

Question to Consider: What do I feel when I consider that God knows everything about me—my fears, my secrets, my heart's deepest longings?

DAY 17

Scripture to Remember: John 17:1–5

Question to Consider: What is the key to eternal life?

DAY 18

Scripture to Remember: Philippians 2:1–11

Question to Consider: Is my attitude the same as Christ's? (How can I become more like Him?)

seven

Finding the Real God of Scripture

The Word of Scripture should never stop sounding in your ears and working in you all day long, just like the words of someone you love. And just as you do not analyze the words of someone you love, but accept them as they are said to you, accept the Word of Scripture and ponder it in your heart, as Mary did. That is all. . . . Do not ask "How shall I pass this on?" but "What does it say to me?" Then ponder this word long in your heart until it has gone right into you and taken possession of you.[1]

—Dietrich Bonhoeffer

I used to have all the answers, just open the Bible and there they were. The truth is, they aren't all there—or if they are, I can't find them. I've tried to convince you that Christianity is logical and straightforward, as if God can be codified and stuffed into files he can't jump out of. Every time uncertainty knocked on the door, I hid behind the couch until it went away. Now I'm the one who's thirsty. My throat was so tight it was painful, my voice strained and hoarse. And the Jesus I've known for twenty years isn't making it go away.[2]

Ever seen a minister lose his cool right in the middle of a Sunday sermon? That's what's happening here to Pastor Chase Falson.

He just can't make sense of the senseless. A little child from his own church has died; *why* did she have to die? One minute she was laughing and riding her bike, but then she fell—and never woke up. *Why* couldn't Chase give some hope to the girl's suffering mom? So much of what he said—so many of his messages—had begun to feel hollow lately.

God is still God, and Chase is still the spiritual leader of an influential Christian church. So what was happening to his faith?

While Chase isn't real—he's the central figure in Ian Morgan Cron's novel *Chasing Francis: A Pilgrim's Tale*—the character's inner turmoil felt real to me. He articulated some of the questions I (Mike) was wrestling with when my faith was stuck, words I wanted to express. Instead, I just read them.

> "And what about our church? I mean, is this all there is? People come in our doors hungry for God, we get them to sign a card that says they believe everything we do, and then we domesticate them." I opened my arms and looked toward the ceiling. "Putnam Hill—Everything You've Come to Expect in a Church and Less," I announced.[3]

A few chapters later, the elders convince Chase to take a leave of absence. "It will do you some good," they suggest. So he sets off on a spiritual pilgrimage—which becomes the reader's pilgrimage too. Seeking to figure out what's gone wrong (and how to get it right again), he turns to his uncle Kenny, a Franciscan priest who lives in Italy.

"Yes, eventually the church became so threatened by modernity's scorn that they turned the Bible into more of a history of ideas rather than a story."

"But why?"

"If they could make all their doctrines string together perfectly and logically, it would make the faith harder to discredit. But the Bible is less about ideas or doctrines than it is a story about people and their up-and-down relationship with God. It's—"

"More a painting than a photograph," I said.

"Right. It's not always clear, it's not black and white, you can't use it forensically in court, it's messy—and like all art, it's open to lots of interpretations," Kenny said.[4]

Now, Scripture isn't a broadly subjective piece of art, even though (for instance) it contains metaphors open to interpretation as well as non-literal or figurative statements (hyperbolic expressions, symbolic terms). Our goal should be to consume each verse carefully, word by word, mindful of not adding to or subtracting from what God says while seeking to hear His message in its right context. Yes, there are some passages that many people don't find completely clear. But many, *many* are plain and straightforward in terms we already understand, and if we come across something that seems elusive or fuzzy, one basic principle is to interpret it in light of what we already know to be true. (That is, its meaning won't contradict anything else God has said to us.)

The fictional Pastor Chase and I were tracking in many ways. Some of his thoughts were mine too.

Yes, life and faith are messy, and they don't always seem to make sense.

Yes, God's Word is a living masterpiece—a passionate love story—yet we often treat it like a legal resource to use as proof of what we believe.

Yes, I also am guilty of trying to stuff God in a box.

Yes, I likewise sometimes view church as more of a "doctrinal enforcement unit" than a community of worship and connection.

Yes, something has gone wrong.

Chasing Life and Missing the Life-Giver

I'd hit a spiritual low point. I felt burned-out and stressed; I felt *stuck*. And like Chase, when uncertainty knocked on the door, I hid behind the couch. Then I readjusted my mask and pretended everything was okay.

At the time, I headed up a youth magazine. I'd been in my position about twenty years and genuinely loved my job. I got to wear the hats of journalist, author, speaker, product developer, event dreamer, creative team leader. I got to travel and meet interesting people from all walks of life. I got to write books and speak on the radio as a "youth-culture expert."

Yet through the years I'd become comfortable. Little by little I was becoming distracted as my title began to swallow up my identity. I started to wonder what had happened to the *real* person inside: child of God, servant of the Most High . . . Christ-follower?

To phrase it another way: *Why hadn't my nose been bloodied for Christ's sake?* I once worked with street kids in L.A. I cared about the broken, the lonely, the homeless. I stood against racism, living among and serving people of different cultures. *How had I gotten soft and sheltered? Why was I content hanging out in the lofty towers of a religious fortress?*

A few months later, after hosting a father-son event in Colorado, a fellow speaker and our camp's worship leader took me aside: "Mike, some of the guys and I have been talking, and we believe God wants us to pray for you."

"Pray? For *me*—what?!" I'd just finished leading three hundred men and boys in prayer. I was the ministry leader, and they wanted to pray for me.

"We all sense that you're really struggling inside," my friend said. "You are holding on, and God wants you to let go. You're trapped; you're full of fear, and you haven't learned to fully trust Him. That, my pal, is nothing short of sin. Your future success in ministry hinges on steps you take right now."

"WHAT?! Let go . . . sin . . . my future?"

My heart was racing, my hands trembling. How could they possibly know these things about me? (I thought I'd pretty well masked my pain.) This was starting to feel like some sort of interventional confrontation. Hearing "God told me something about your future," well, that freaks me out. I'd normally run—but there they were, surrounding me, laying hands on me.

Quit being phony. It's time to be real—time to surrender control. Let go.

I prayed with the guys, cried a little, and confessed a few things: my lack of trust in God *and* people; my tendency to please others before the Lord; and yes, my fear of uncertainty—especially about where Christ was leading me.

I wish I could say I changed course that day, but I didn't. (More like I took a half step.)

Not long afterward, I slipped back into my routine with life's pressures and distractions. Call me hardheaded, a slow learner . . . I'm certain I'd fit right in with the grumblers Moses tried to lead into the Promised Land! But one morning, as I sat in my office, I took a look around and smiled. *I like this place. I like what I do. I like who I am. More important, I love my family. I'm really happy.* (In other words, "I want to leave things just as they are because I'm too afraid to allow myself or my family to try something new.")

I bowed my head and began to pray: "I don't fully get what happened at the retreat or what to do with it. Frankly, the whole thing scares me. Thank you for this magazine and this ministry. Thank you for your many blessings. Thank you for—"

"But are you challenged?"

I stopped midsentence, opened my eyes, and looked around. I was alone, but I'm not exaggerating in saying those words ripped through my mind like an audible voice.

Am I challenged? What does that mean?

I was not, in fact, experiencing challenge. I saw my life as manageable—within my control—and that's how I liked it. But what I preferred really wasn't the point, because being a Christ-follower (let alone a ministry leader) means I can't pitch a tent in a comfort zone. I know that God wants to move me along in my faith—on to deeper things, new challenges, more growth.

Whether I liked it or not, everything was about to change.

———

Eighteen months after the mountaintop retreat, the economy went south. In November 2008, the mega-sized ministry I called my place of employment had to downsize by half. My magazine was cut; I was tossed from the fortress.

I was terrified.

There were more tears . . . and many, many more prayers.

One Sunday, as my family and I were heading home from church, I was deep in thought when I realized that God had reached forth His awakening hand—through His Word and through the words of others—and was guiding me by His firm touch on my shoulder.

He'd done it through a tender question from my little boy: "Daddy, will you get to be with Jesus in heaven?" *I was wrestling with doubt.*

He'd done it through a loving embrace from my wife: "You do know things will be okay—don't you?" *I was weary and on the verge of spiritual burnout.*

He'd done it through the concern of my friend Lance: "How are you doing today—I mean, really doing, on the inside?" *I was afraid to be honest.*

He'd done it through Scripture: "Because you are luke-warm—neither hot nor cold—I am about to spit you out of my mouth."[5] *I was disconnected from God but didn't want to admit it or face up to it.*

———

Then—not right away, not in an instant, but over some time and through a process—something I hadn't dreamed would happen actually happened. I came to experience the certainty of "being okay." I *felt* God's peace. I *knew* He truly can be trusted.

I'd been establishing myself as an author, and writing projects were starting to land. Pondering the question He had asked, as it came back to me, I had the realization that *no—I wasn't being challenged, I'd been comfortable. Now I'm challenged and anything but comfortable.* Yet I felt more alive than ever. I was excited, even; terrified, yet excited—I saw the opportunity to move on, to move forward, to grow.

———

So, where are we headed now, Lord?

He took me someplace I never expected—back to the Bible! Not the ministry just yet; right into the pages of His Word, which I'd so often neglected and misunderstood (relying heavily on other people's opinions).

I'll never forget a friend once asking, "Have you ever read the Bible all the way through?"

I couldn't say *yes.*

She continued: "I'm a Christ-follower, yet I haven't made the Bible a daily part of my life. . . . What if Christianity isn't what I think it is? What if it's better? What if my image of God isn't the right one? I really want the truth, so I'm trying not to read any other books as I focus on the Bible."

That advice opened my eyes, and God began a transformational work in me. He wasn't leading me into *Bible reading*—He was compelling me to *engage* His message to me with a lover's passion. He was showing me how to find my Savior in His pages . . . how to have "a daily walk with Jesus."

Without even knowing the concept, I was finally getting Powered by Four.

———✦———

Near the end of *Chasing Francis,* the newly rejuvenated Pastor Chase returns to his church with a fresh outlook:

> When I left here, I wasn't sure what a Christian looked like anymore. My idea of what it meant to follow Jesus had run out of gas. I started feeling less like a pastor and more like a salesman of a consumerized Jesus I didn't believe in. Learning about Francis [of Assisi] helped me fall in love with Jesus again—and with the church again, too.[6]

This protagonist and I had so much in common. While I didn't hop on a plane to Italy or chase the trail of a long-ago spiritual pilgrim, I too was finally encountering the one true God of the Scriptures. I found Him in His Word.

I was no longer afraid to open up the pages. Engaging the Bible was no longer a dreaded chore. I was falling in love with the Lord's call on my life:

God authorized and commanded me to commission you: Go out and train everyone you meet, far and near, in this way of life, marking them by baptism in the threefold name: Father, Son, and Holy Spirit. Then instruct them in the practice of all I have commanded you. I'll be with you as you do this, day after day after day, right up to the end of the age.[7]

Mostly, I was falling in love with God again.

Head to unstuck.gotandem.com for more of Mike's story and some free downloadable resources to help get you, your study group, and/or your church moving toward spiritual breakthrough.

———◉———

Exactly how did the Powered by Four Solution change the way Mike connects with God's Word—and connects with God through His Word? How can you begin applying it to your daily walk? In the next chapter, Arnie walks you through some specifics.

———◉———

Research Reveals: The truth of 2 Timothy 3:16 was put to the test in a random sample of 2,967 teens and adults who engaged the Bible four or more times a week. They reported a deeper relationship with God and also showed improved moral behaviors.

Encouraging Nudge: Like sheep, we tend to drift away from our Shepherd. Yet with a firm grasp of the Bible, nurtured through daily engagement, our ability to hear God's voice and understand His will is strengthened.

Spiritual
Stepping Stones

● *DAy 19*

Scripture to Remember: John 8:31–32

Question to Consider: Is truth setting me free?

● *DAy 20*

Scripture to Remember: 2 Timothy 3:10–17

Question to Consider: Do I believe the Holy Bible is God's infallible and authoritative Word? (Why, or why not?)

● *DAy 21*

Scripture to Remember: 2 Peter 1:12–21

Question to Consider: Am I allowing the Holy Spirit to speak to me through Scripture? If so, am I endeavoring to *live* God's Word?

eight

Vertical Conversations

Bible reading is a means of listening to and obeying God, not gathering religious data by which we can be our own gods. You are going to hear stories in this Book that will take you out of your preoccupation with yourself and into the spacious freedom in which God is working the world's salvation. You are going to come across words and sentences that stab you awake to a beauty and hope that will connect you with your real life.[1]

—Eugene H. Peterson

Henrietta Mears was a brilliant scholar who wasn't known for mincing words. Some found her remarks a bit stinging, but I (Arnie) kind of liked that about her. When it came to our most important relationship—connecting intimately with our Lord and Savior Jesus Christ—she had a way of cutting through wordy theologies and complicated doctrines, and she got right to the heart of what we must do: "If we are going to know the Bible, we must give time to it and arrange for it. We must adjust our lives so that time is made. Unless we do, we shall never come into any worthy knowledge of the Word."[2]

Years ago I determined to stop making excuses and start making time. As you've read, Mike took that gutsy step too. And the more the two of us grow along the way, the more sensitive we become to the challenges of life today. We feel an urgency to keep our relationship with Jesus on solid footing. Now more than ever we all need to hear from God and draw closer to Him.

Lukewarm spirituality just doesn't cut it. Actually, *lukewarm* and *spiritual* are like oil and water. Christ-followers are either on the path with their Lord and Savior or off the path altogether—there's no in-between. Only those "who know their God shall be strong, and carry out great exploits" for Him.[3] The Bible is the key to growing us each day.

When I launched into Scripture, I soon became aware of the enemy's forces working to discourage me and block my efforts.[4] Satan tried tripping me up with time-wasters (TV, movies, frivolous shopping), tried getting me to cling to negative emotions (fear, worry, insecurity), tried turning my focus to old wounds and past sins so I'd question my ability to follow Christ.

"Voices" of distraction and dissent began buzzing loudly, attempting to drown out God's voice. *"The Bible is an outdated rule book." "There are more effective ways of connecting with God." "The Scriptures are inaccurate, inconsistent, and irrelevant for today's believer." "All of this was written for a specific culture for use in a specific period of human history."*

My response was to remind myself what I believe about the Bible and to consider carefully the lenses I was looking through. I embraced what it says about itself: "The word of the Lord is right and true; he is faithful in all he does."[5] Billy Graham, long known as our nation's pastor, said:

The Bible is old; yet it is ever new. It is the most modern book in the world today. There is a false notion that a book as ancient as the Bible cannot speak to modern needs. People somehow think that in an age of scientific achievement, when knowledge has increased more in the past twenty-five years than in all preceding centuries put together, this ancient Book is out-of-date. But to all who read and love the Bible, it is relevant for our generation.[6]

The *Powered by Four Solution* has made a difference in how we receive Scripture daily, and it's helping Christians worldwide. Before we get started with it, let's take a look at what this concept *is* and *isn't*. It all truly boils down to three simple principles:

We stop reading the Bible and start engaging it.

It's essential that we receive, reflect on, and respond to God's Word consistently.

We pay close attention to frequency of Bible engagement.

Engaging Scripture four-plus times a week makes the biggest difference.

We consider what the Bible is.

God's Word to us is how we hear from and share two-way conversation with our Creator. It's our personal connection.

First, a few questions:

Why engage "at least four times a week"? (Isn't that a formula?) Relationships need consistent connections in order to grow. We grow closer to loved ones by spending time with them. It's the same with Christ.

Why the focus on changing negative behaviors? (Isn't that just another plan to be moral, not free?) Real faith isn't about a swap of bad behaviors for good ones. It is, as we've said, about a thriving *relationship* with Jesus. We all struggle with something, and we all battle sin daily; however, the fact is, when we grow, our choices and actions do change.

Why focus on the Bible . . . and why this method? The Word of God is transformational—it's His living, breathing message to us. When we engage—not just read—the Holy Scriptures, our hearts are changed.

How to Be Powered by Four

With the key elements (above) in mind, here's a meaningful way in which we apply this solution. Again, there's no ten-step plan everyone should follow precisely. I've presented some steps that work for me. Consider a handful of ideas and then mix in your own style. Bible engagement is personal and vital.

Change the way we approach God.

When Grandma hands us a Bible and says, "Read this," she means well, and her heart's in the right place, yet merely reading just doesn't work for most of us. Our guilty conscience kicks in; we know we should do it, but usually we don't. As for study plans, well, Grandma likes those too. We've found that while half of American believers over age sixty use one, only one-fourth of those under forty do so.

For me, the word *study* often got in the way. I'd either rush through my so-called quiet time (usually because I felt too busy to take time to study), I'd skip opening my Bible and read other people's thoughts about Scripture, or I'd pick-and-choose my way through God's Word, cramming verses into my head as if preparing for a test. Reading this way left me exhausted and frustrated—anything but refreshed. I certainly wasn't growing spiritually.

Instead of approaching devotional times with primarily an info-gathering mindset, I've been learning how to *engage* Scripture, looking for *connection, relationship,* and *spiritual transformation.* This enables my heart and soul to receive intimate words from God.

As I receive passages:

I listen intently, relationally, to God's personal message for me (rather than seeking to learn more about Him cognitively).

I allow God's Word to become an instrument of His control (rather than a tool to accomplish my own goals).

Savor and wrestle with Scripture to engage it.

Engage is a word with multiple meanings. *Webster's*[7] defines it this way:

to draw into; involve; to attract and hold; to keep busy; occupy; to enter into a conflict with; to interlock with; mesh together; to entangle; to pledge oneself; promise; undertake; agree; to occupy or involve oneself; take part; be active.

Each description captures various phases of our time spent in the Bible.

As we draw into God's Word, His message takes hold of our minds and emotions; it occupies our souls. Inevitably our stubborn human will pushes us into a conflict with the Holy Spirit. We interlock with Him and wrestle with a concept or a command, often feeling the sting of a guilty conscience.

How can I forgive and turn the other cheek after what they did to me?

Be holy as you are holy? Lord, you know my secrets; you know the things that hold me back. I'm not even sure I'm cut out to be a Christ-follower.

What do you mean, "There's a log in my eye"?

Ultimately God wins. Getting entangled with truth untangles sin. And if we surrender control to Christ, our will begins to mesh with His. We pledge ourselves to a new way of relating to others and come into agreement with God. Our faith activates. We're moving, and we're growing.

Engaging God's Word is the process of learning to think and love biblically. Here are keys that can unlock transformation.

Receive God's Word

> We genuinely take God's Word into our
> minds by "spiritually consuming" the
> words of the Bible as we read or listen.

Eugene H. Peterson, who spent years translating and paraphrasing Scripture into a user-friendly rendering we know as *The Message,* says:

> Words spoken or written to us under the metaphor of eating, words to be freely taken in, tasted, chewed, savored, swallowed, and digested, have a very different effect on us from those that come at us from the outside, whether in the form of propaganda or information.[8]

Receiving Scripture is *much* more than gathering facts. Have we really expected knowledge to give us eternal life? Many, like the Pharisees, have memorized and "mastered" entire texts while failing to experience the truths found in God's Word. As Henry Blackaby reminds us:

> It is a subtle temptation to prefer the book to the Author. A book will not confront you about your sin; the Author will. Books can be ignored; it is much harder to avoid the Author when He is seeking a relationship with you.[9]

Power by Four is about *metabolizing* Scripture, allowing God's message to become ours, inviting His life to surge through us. We want a deeper relationship with Jesus—to know Him better, walk with Him, become like Him. God's life-giving words help us do this, writes Ruth Haley Barton:

> When we engage the Scriptures for spiritual transformation . . . we engage not only our mind but also our heart, our emotions, our body, our curiosity, our imagination and our will. We open ourselves to a deeper level of understanding and insight that grows out of and leads us deeper into our personal relationship with the One behind the text. And it is in the context of relational intimacy that real life change takes place.[10]

Receiving the Word of God doesn't mean simply flipping open a bound book and giving our eyes a workout. It can involve our ears too. Be creative (don't formulize; personalize), and pursue engagement as a want-to (not a have-to) connection with God.

For multiple "touches," try interacting with His Word through different and various options technology offers. The marketplace holds myriad products and programs; we're especially partial to our Bible-engagement tool called "goTandem," by which participants receive Scripture throughout the day in ways that fit their lifestyle. Some receive voice messages; others get texts; you can choose e-mails that contain passages as well as nuggets that speak directly to current personal challenges; you can request weekly phone calls from a Spiritual Growth Encourager.

Tandem's goal is to avoid one-size-fits-all plans. Christ-followers are free to mature and grow as God wants to accomplish it. Three simple steps launch a customized path:

STEP 1: An online (absolutely confidential) spiritual-growth assessment. This fifteen-minute-or-so questionnaire helps the CBE professionals develop a spiritual growth plan to fit your individual needs.

STEP 2: After assessment, you'll be notified about receipt of the questionnaire and then sent an e-mail requesting personal- and message-preference information. You can even select day and time to receive your own weekly encouragement call.

STEP 3: When you receive your chosen content, engage and grow!

Check it out for yourself at www.unstuck.gotandem.com.

Reflect on God's Word

> We actively ponder God's words
> into our heart and soul.

Reflection (or meditation) is an active consideration of biblical truth that, again, the Bible directly tells us to undertake: "Be transformed by the renewing of your mind. Then you will be able to test and approve what God's will is—his good, pleasing and perfect will."[11]

Reflection fosters understanding, and understanding enables us to hear God's personal message. Let me demonstrate with an example. Take a close look at Christ's words in Luke 6:46–49:

> Why do you call me, "Lord, Lord," and do not do what I say? As for everyone who comes to me and hears my words and puts them into practice, I will show you what they are like. They are like a man building a house, who dug down deep and laid the foundation on rock. When a flood came, the torrent struck that house but could not shake it, because it was well built. But the one who hears my words and does not put them into practice is like a man who built a house on the ground without a foundation. The moment the torrent struck that house, it collapsed and its destruction was complete.

Now go back and read the passage a couple more times, *meditating* on what He's saying. Pull it apart sentence by sentence and *listen* to His voice, His heart. Invite and allow His Spirit to speak to you.

Ponder His words on an intellectual level: What is the main message here? Is He giving a warning? A promise? A command? What is He teaching about God's character? What is He saying about my eternal destiny?

Ponder His words on a relational level: How do they apply uniquely to me? Is He calling me to action? Is He reminding me to slow down? Listen more? Is He encouraging me? Is He disciplining me? Have I been neglecting Him? Neglecting others?

Then get more personal:

- *"Here's how I feel about these verses. . . ."*
- *"Here's what's hard for me, God. . . ."*
- *"Help me understand, because I don't get this. . . ."*
- *"Help me move from my way of thinking to your way. . . ."*

145

Seek to apply: "Lord, what do you want me to *do* with these words?"

Through the process of Bible engagement we . . .

. . . enable God's Word to shape our thinking and sharpen our ability to understand His will. Daniel[12] and Mary[13] offer prime examples of reflection on God's Word as essential to spiritual growth. When they faced situations in which they couldn't figure out what God was doing, instead of giving up they did their best to ponder carefully. Their actions remind us to submit to God's wisdom even when His work doesn't seem to make sense to us.

. . . saturate our mind with Scripture, which can help us battle temptation and sin. It will help us increasingly to think as God does, which will help us obey Him and do His will. Our obedience will eventually turn into desire!

Biblical meditation is the thoughtful contemplation of God's Word and reflecting on Him in the person and work of Jesus Christ. It's a powerful tool when joined with prayer and Bible reading. Meditation needn't be (as some religions teach) an emptying of the mind for relaxation or another self-serving result. Biblical meditation requires focus—active mental engagement coupled with emotional energy—and it's absolutely worth it.

Respond to God's Word

> We look for ways to live out the
> truth as revealed in the Bible.

This is where spiritual growth really begins. Having received Scripture, and having spent ample time reflecting on it, pondering it into our lives, we get our faith moving by *responding* to it. Flip back just a few pages and reread about defining the word *engage*; here's where we may end up interlocking with and wrestling with a concept or a command. But if we surrender control to God and step forward in faith, our wills do begin to mesh with His.

Little by little we grow. Step by step God works His sanctification in us. Jesus says, "Give Me all of you. Not just your time, your work, or your money. I want *you*. I'll give you a new self—*My*self. I will become yours."

C. S. Lewis noted that only God can do everything needful in our souls.

> The New Testament . . . talks about Christians "being born again" . . . about "putting on Christ"; about Christ "being formed in us"; about our coming to "have the mind of Christ."
>
> Put right out of your head the idea that these are only fancy ways of saying that Christians are to read what Christ said and try to carry it out—as a man may read what Plato or Marx said and try to carry it out. They mean something much more than that. They mean that a real Person, Christ, here and now, in that very room where you are saying your prayers, is doing things in you. It is not a question of a good man who died two thousand years ago. It is a living Man, still as much a man as you, and still as much God as He was when He created the world, really coming and interfering with your very self; killing the old natural self in you and replacing it with the kind of self He has. At first, only for moments. Then for longer periods. Finally, if all goes well, turning you permanently into a different sort of thing; into a new little Christ, a being which, in its own small way, has the same kind of life as God; which shares in His power, joy, knowledge, and eternity.[14]

In regard to our example of Jesus' words in Luke 6:46–49, consider a story Mike shared with me.

After he received this passage into his heart and mind and had chewed on it awhile, he began feeling proud of himself. *I've laid my foundation on rock*, he thought. *No worries of a torrent wiping out my faith.*

But after a heart-to-heart conversation with Jesus, he sensed discomfort deep in his gut. Then a guilty conscience kicked in. *Lord, are you saying I'm not listening to you? Are there cracks in my faith? Am I doubting you?*

More reflection. More questions. Then Mike interlocked with the Spirit of Christ and wrestled with the hard facts. Jesus was showing him how fear and worry were still at work in his life. Instead of trusting Him and stepping out in faith with a particular issue, he'd maintained a controlling grip and was trying to handle it himself. He wasn't hearing God's message and putting it into practice—he was heading his own way "without a foundation." Had a "torrent" struck, he would have experienced nothing short of destruction.

At first Mike tried to excuse his actions and resisted the Lord's direction. But his back was against the wall; he was frustrated and weary from the fight. He knew God would have His way. He knew the right choice was to come clean with his struggles.

Next came surrender. Then confession and repentance. Then . . . growth.

We don't yet see things clearly. We're squinting in a fog, peering through a mist. But it won't be long before the weather clears and the sun shines bright! We'll see it all then, see it all as clearly as God sees us, knowing him directly just as he knows us! But for right now, until that completeness, we have three things to do to lead us toward that consummation: Trust steadily in God, hope unswervingly, love extravagantly. And the best of the three is love.[15]

When the Bible Doesn't Make Sense

"What should I do if I encounter something I just don't understand?"

The answer can take entire books and courses to describe accurately for serious Bible students. What about the rest of us regular folks? How can we receive, reflect upon, and respond to God's Word when we're confused?

We took our curiosity to Dr. Mary Spaulding who received her PhD in Biblical Studies from University of Manchester. She teaches courses on this subject as well as Hebrew, serving as an adjunct faculty member at Nazarene Bible College and Fuller Theological Seminary (both in Colorado Springs). Dr. Spaulding periodically teaches college programs throughout Africa. She shared this overview of a technique that helps her:

When I come across a passage that I don't understand, I try always to take the following steps:

First, I ask God for His wisdom and direction, and then I research the passage. The Holy Spirit can guide and direct in various ways but does not usually provide concrete information about a subject. I must do the hard work of research alongside the Spirit's more subtle guidance. How I research the passage depends upon the particular issue I do not understand.

If the problem is the use of a word or phrase in the passage, then I will seek out the original Greek or Hebrew behind the English. This involves studying the Greek/Hebrew word's full range of meaning, its general cultural usage at the time of the writing, its use elsewhere in the Bible, and the author's use of that word in his other biblical writings and in the rest of the book in which the passage is found. The final step then is to determine the meaning that is most appropriate to the word's immediate context. The immediate context is the most important determinant of meaning for any word we use, and our assumption must be that the author had one meaning in mind when he placed that word in its particular sentence within the passage.

If the problem deals with a custom, expectation, or behavior of the time, then I will turn to a larger Bible encyclopedia. I also use a background commentary, and/or a specific commentary on the Bible book in which the passage is found. Reviewing what is written about the passage in more than one resource or commentary can be very helpful in determining controversial passages that are being interpreted today in more than one way. Controversial passages must be handled much more carefully and thoroughly in order to glean the underlying points of argument among contemporary scholars.

If it's an important concept to understand, I may also look for modern-day books written specifically about that issue. In addition . . . many of the Jewish and Greek writings of the time (e.g., Josephus, the Dead Sea Scrolls, the Pseudepigrapha) can give us more direct information about the people and their practices and beliefs at the time of the writing of the particular Bible book in which the passage is found. I also keep in mind that something being discussed in the New Testament may have its explanation and roots in the Old Testament. Sometimes the Bible has the answer to our puzzles within its own pages.

When researching an issue, I try not to use modern resources more than a few decades old. Why? The scholarly world is constantly gaining new insights about the Bible through further research about ancient times. I do not turn to websites for information unless I know the site and its author well; there's a tremendous amount of incorrect and misleading information online. Also, free online commentaries usually are no longer under copyright protection because of their age and, therefore, may contain inaccurate information. Building up one's own research library or having access to a Bible college or seminary library is extremely helpful to an in-depth and thorough study of Scripture.[16]

When It Seems There Isn't Time to Engage the Bible

"I want to grow spiritually, but what should I do if I don't have time for something like Powered by Four?"

There simply are no shortcuts to spiritual growth. The way to life—to God—is vigorous and requires total attention.[17] But again, many people do benefit from multiple Scripture "touches" throughout the day. Bible tools often are helpful.

Dr. Woodrow Kroll, president of Back to the Bible, is passionate about helping people engage God's Word:

> When time is short, a quick bite as you go out the door may have to do. But if you really want to enjoy a meal, you need to slow down and taste it. It works the same way with finding God in the Bible. It's easy for us to go to the Bible for a "quick bite" every now and then without stopping to truly taste it.
>
> How do we taste God in the Bible? We take it in and savor every bit of it. Approach the Bible the same way you would approach a good meal—go slow, take time, and enjoy every part of it.
>
> Take a Scripture passage from 2 Samuel 22, for example. You won't get much of a picture of God if you speed through it. But read it again, and look at all the metaphors David uses in this song. God is a rock. What's rock-like about God? God is a fortress. How is God like a fortress? God is a Savior. What are you being saved from?
>
> By stopping to "taste" the Bible—really taking it in and savoring it—we learn to trust God in a whole new way. As we meditate (*literally* "to chew") on God's Word, we go beyond mere sight to understanding.[18]

A Better Way to Grow

Recap: When my team and I asked tens of thousands to describe their spiritual lives, we got an earful! Our questions included how they communicate with God, what helps their faith to grow, what holds them back, how often they do or don't read the Bible, and more. Careful analysis of a select sample of Christ-following adults unearthed the facts we've emphasized: Engaging the Bible four or more times a week makes a difference in how we think, live, grow, and relate to God and others.

Here's what some said about God's Word:

"I find God in the Scriptures, and He speaks to me in a personal way."

"It helps me overcome temptation."

"It gives me hope."

"It gives me truth."

"God is healing old wounds as I meet with Him for prayer and study."

"God's Word gives me a fresh insight every day."

"I'm learning how to forgive."

"I'm learning how to trust again."

"I feel more alive as I receive Scripture into my heart and mind."

"My prayer life is much more meaningful."

"God renews my mind through Scripture."

"I'm beginning to understand God's will for my life."

Powered by Four is helping many Christ-followers get unstuck spiritually and align their lives with God's will. They're growing and thriving and changing in significant ways.

Engaging the Bible also helps us to confidently share the gospel, and it motivates our involvement in ministry outreach. Those who regularly immerse in it are 228 percent more likely to share their faith with others, 231 percent more likely to disciple others, and 407 percent more likely to memorize Scripture.

In the next chapter, we'll share why the Bible isn't "another religious text" or "the ultimate rule book," and describe how to engage God's Word through "the lenses of reality."

Research Reveals: Receiving Scripture daily—along with reflecting on it and responding to it—transforms us. We can expect (1) direction from God, (2) the ability to discern His truth from competing voices, (3) freedom from wrong thinking, and (4) a way to withstand temptation.

Encouraging Nudge: Being firmly grounded in God's Word enables us to grow spiritually and draws us closer to Christ. Intimacy with Him is cultivated through consistent Bible engagement.

Take a look at unstuck.gotandem.com for more practical ways to grow spiritually. Do this every day during your forty-five-day journey.

Spiritual
Stepping Stones

● **DAY 22**

Scripture to Remember: Hebrews 4:12

Question to Consider: Am I chewing on God's Word—allowing it to penetrate my heart and to search out my motivations? (Am I engaging Scripture, not just reading it?)

● DAY 23

Scripture to Remember: Psalm 119:89–104

Question to Consider: Am I pondering God's Word—meditating on it and committing it to memory? If not, when and how will I begin doing this? (This is a good time to set some goals.)

● DAY 24

Scripture to Remember: John 5:36–40

Question to Consider: Am I responding to God's Word—learning how to live it daily—in loving Jesus, laying down my life for others, and moving into abundant life one step at a time?

nine

Giant Squid
and Bible Truth

Don't trifle with the Bible. . . . Don't wish to put on colored glasses of people's opinions and then read through the interpretation put on it by other minds. Let the Spirit of God Himself teach you. We all have a right to read it for ourselves. "No prophecy of Scripture came about by the prophet's own interpretation" (2 Peter 1:20). Read it seeking for illumination. It is a revelation and He will flash light upon the page as you come humbly.[1]

—Dr. Henrietta C. Mears

"Have you ever read the Bible all the way through?"

"How do these ancient writings change people today?"

"Is the Bible kind of like a rule book we're supposed to follow?"

"Why are some passages so violent and cruel?"

"Why do certain verses seem confusing and contradictory?"

"Is Bible reading the only way we grow spiritually?"

"Does God speak only through His Word?"

"Can we skip the Bible and still get to heaven?"

With each mouse-click, question after question about the Bible popped up on my (Mike's) screen—along with endless streams of answers.

"The Bible's a constrained collection of regional folklore," one wrote.

"It's ambiguous, seething with ignorance, and doesn't relate to Western culture," answered another person.

Somebody with the user name "Wonder Weirdo" insisted that the only way to read Scripture is with "a grain of salt and a shot of tequila."

"Are they serious?" I said aloud. "The questions are honest, but these so-called answers are just plain—"

"Squid, Dad. Giant squid . . . remember?"

My concentration was broken by my impatient third-grader. Christopher held up his homework assignment and tapped on the words *sea creatures*. "I need scary pictures of monster squid. I need to know what they eat, how big they get, where they live. That's what my report is about—not the Bible."

I smiled. "And we'll find lots of squid stuff, I'm sure of it. I just got sidetracked with what people are saying. Some of it's pretty mean."

"*Mean?* About the Bible?!" His young mind couldn't fathom such a thought. "But it's from God . . . and He's not mean."

"Not everyone gets that," I explained, groping for the right words. "And some people don't think God's Word can help us. Instead, they call it a bunch of boring rules and say it's confusing and outdated."

He squinted. I could tell the wheels in his head were spinning wildly. "The Bible is how God talks to us. He tells us important stuff about Him . . . and how we should live. But He doesn't make us read it. And He doesn't make us believe in Him. We have to choose."

I nearly fell out of my chair. My boy nailed it—perfectly summed up heady theology. Yes, God talks to us through Scripture, and there's a lot we need to hear. But He doesn't force it on anyone. It's up to us to slow down, put away our misconceptions, dig in, tune in, and experience it for ourselves.

How did an Internet search for monster squid take us to God's Word?

It started on a Q&A site that invites users to "share knowledge" and "be an expert." In the middle of the home page—right next to questions about cooking turkeys and curing hiccups—were ten words that leapt off the page: *"Have you ever read the Bible all the way through?"*

I couldn't resist.

What was buzzing around about God and the Bible? After all, this site claimed more than two hundred million users worldwide. What would I find?

More than 68,000 posts about God, the Bible, and specifically, *Bible reading!* By comparison, when I entered *giant squid,* only three hundred comments surfaced. Sadly, though, user info about *Loligo pealei* and *Ommastrephes* (squid) was far more accurate than the comments on the Bible.

I saw virtual reams of raging rants against Christianity or the church and irreverent jabs at God's Word. I read some bumper-sticker quotes from well-meaning folks. Here and there I'd unearth something of a gem, but most answers were thin on knowledge and fat (obese, honestly) with opinion.

The Many-Hued Glasses of Opinion

We all know websites that are more entertaining than in-formative; hopefully we're able to take what we read with a grain of salt and a shot of prune juice. We need to be plugged in to the Source of truth, the yardstick by which life's most important questions can be measured.

In regard to those questions—the ones God's Word ad-dresses—there are a few we likewise have been seeking to tackle, such as, Why do so many of us lose the day spiritually to the point of never sensing God's presence or rarely helping others? Why isn't the truth capturing our hearts and minds and, thus, directing our steps? Why do we keep getting stuck spiritually?

For Christ-followers, the answers often have been hard to admit.

As we've seen, many of us are confused about Scripture—what it is and how to use it. And even more of us are chopping it up into bits and pieces and reading through the lenses of our own opinions and preferences, which can seriously distort God's heart for us.

Furthermore, a lot of believers are living "squinty-eyed," which Jesus calls a lethal mistake:

> Your eyes are windows into your body. If you open your eyes wide in wonder and belief, your body fills up with light. If you live squinty-eyed in greed and distrust, your body is a dank cellar. If you pull the blinds on your windows, what a dark life you will have![2]

He came to heal the blind—that includes you and me.[3] And He tells us, "Whoever has ears, let them hear."[4]

By now you're well aware of a widespread problem: So many Christians today aren't engaging the Bible. Instead of entering in on their own, they've been gravitating toward books *about* Scripture, relying on other people's opinions. They aren't hearing directly from God through His Word. This is weakening the church.

First, pastors and theologians agree the United States isn't the predominantly Christian nation it once was, and Bible-believing churches are no longer the hubs of family life. In fact, those who aren't Christ-followers are rapidly becoming less and less a fringe segment of our society.[5] What's more, their faith's influence on culture and individual lives is barely visible. "Contemporary Americans are hard pressed to identify any specific value added," explains George Barna. "Partly due to the nature of today's media, they have no problem identifying the faults of the churches and Christian people."[6]

Some of this, of course, is good. We've taken some rightfully placed criticism the last thirty years about becoming off track in our goal to show the light of truth to the world. We *have* needed to make adjustments and changes.

Second, though, our tepid approach to faith is affecting a generation of future leaders. About 40 percent of those between sixteen and twenty-nine are avowedly rejecting the Bible and Christianity. Among the generations known as Mosaics (born 1984–2002) and Busters (born 1965–1983), many use words like *hypocritical, insensitive,* and *judgmental* to describe the church. David Kinnaman says Christianity has "an image problem" among young Americans; those outside the church are skeptical about all things *Christian*: the faith itself, the people who profess it, the Bible, and Jesus Christ.

> Those inside the church see it as well—especially Christians in their twenties and thirties. They are bringing up some of the same challenges, questions, and doubts facing those outside the church. . . .
>
> [As for the latter,] their impressions of the Bible are mixed: most think it has good values, but only three out of ten believe that it is accurate in all the principles it teaches.[7]

Third, whatever our age and whatever the condition of our faith, we're all impacted by convincing voices—public opinion, media, friends, relatives, colleagues. Also, the material and virtual worlds are so intertwined as to challenge our separation of fact from fantasy. When blogs bash believers, when the masses marginalize the Bible, it's not hard to get caught up in what's popular. Though there's no necessary connection between a majority (or even unanimous) vote and what's right, it takes courage—and more—to withstand and turn against a tide of opposition. Tempting, seemingly palatable thoughts surface: *Maybe the Bible is more a part of the problem than the solution. . . . Maybe there really are better ways to know God intimately. . . .*

We shove Scripture aside for something less demanding and much more PC. Trying to justify our choice, we might even beef up prayer, join spiritual formation groups, and plunge into every fad or formula we can grab. Before we know it, our wheels are spinning, our growth comes to a halt, and guess what?

We're miserable again.

Fortunately, miraculously, our heavenly Father *never* gives up on us. As Frank Laubach reminds us, "God comes with His awakening hand, takes us by the shoulders and gives us a thorough awakening."[8]

When He comes, *we'd* be wise to wake up and refocus. Are you in the midst of a spiritual shake-up? Is it time to change your lenses?

The Lenses of Reality

A simple yet crucial step helped me start navigating through my faith fog and got me beginning to grow again: I had to reconsider (then exchange) the lenses through which I'd been looking. As I wrestled with what I believe—about the identity and character of God, the unquenchability of Christ's love for me, the complete effectiveness of His atonement for my sins, the certainty of everlasting life, the without-ceasing importance of confession and prayer, the nature and the necessity of Scripture, the foundations of spiritual growth, and much, much more—I began to discern and discover truth I'd missed while wearing the wrong glasses.

And I found it by going to the place I'd stayed away from (or only gone for drive-thru service).

The Bible itself.

The Bible is all about relationship.

I will instruct you and teach you in the way you should go; I will counsel you with my loving eye on you.[9]

Pay attention to what I say; turn your ear to my words. Do not let them out of your sight, keep them within your heart; for they are life to those who find them and health to one's whole body.[10]

The Word became flesh and made his dwelling among us. We have seen his glory, the glory of the one and only Son, who came from the Father, full of grace and truth.[11]

J. I. Packer wrote:

God's purpose in revelation is to make friends with us. God's friendship with men and women begins and grows through speech. His to us in revelation, and ours to Him in prayer and praise. Though I cannot see God, He and I can yet be personal friends, because in revelation He talks to me.[12]

The Bible is God's living Word.

Everywhere Scripture is packed with God's power. Receiving His message is like having His very breath breathed into us.

Heaven and earth will pass away, but my words will never pass away.[13]

The word of God is alive and active. Sharper than any double-edged sword, it penetrates even to dividing soul and spirit, joints and marrow; it judges the thoughts and attitudes of the heart. Nothing in all creation is hidden from God's sight. Everything is uncovered and laid bare before the eyes of him to whom we must give account.[14]

We also have the prophetic message as something completely reliable, and you will do well to pay attention to it, as to a light shining in a dark place, until the day dawns and the morning star rises in your hearts. Above all, you must understand that no prophecy of Scripture came about by the prophet's own interpretation of things. For prophecy never had its origin in the human will, but prophets, though human, spoke from God as they were carried along by the Holy Spirit.[15]

The Bible is God's story.

Through beginnings and endings, sin and salvation, heaven and hell, spiritual battles and eternal victory, each of us is taking part in the narrative of this one book, one story—*His* story.[16]

By the word of the Lord the heavens were made, their starry host by the breath of his mouth.[17]

In the beginning was the Word, and the Word was with God, and the Word was God. He was with God in the beginning. Through him all things were made; without him nothing was made that has been made. In him was life, and that life was the light of all mankind. The light shines in the darkness, and the darkness has not overcome it.[18]

You have been born again, not of perishable seed, but of imperishable, through the living and enduring word of God. For, "All people are like grass, and all their glory is like the flowers of the field; the grass withers and the flowers fall, but the word of the Lord endures forever."[19]

The Bible is the answer to our spiritual growth.

"The first-century disciples were totally involved with a Person," Richard Halverson explains. "They were followers of Jesus. They were learners of Jesus. They were committed to Jesus."[20] Our faith grows as we encounter Jesus in the Bible. The message of Scripture is the One who is "the way and the truth and the life."[21]

Faith comes from hearing the message, and the message is heard through the word about Christ.[22]

Continue in what you have learned and have become convinced of, because you know those from whom you learned it, and how from infancy you have known the Holy Scriptures, which are able to make you wise for salvation through faith in Christ Jesus. All Scripture is God-breathed and is useful for teaching, rebuking, correcting and training in righteousness, so that the servant of God may be thoroughly equipped for every good work.[23]

A Better Way to See

These are the lenses through which we're all meant to see.

God's Word is the foundation of our faith. It's how we connect with our Creator and grow spiritually. It's the key to keeping our lives anchored during times of turmoil. And as we've learned how to *engage* Scripture, we almost feel we're experiencing the Bible again for the first time.

163

We no longer see the Bible as "the ultimate rule book."

Like many, we had been caught up in do's and don'ts, thinking that faith was about combating our desires and "striving to be good Christians." *If I only do this and never do that, maybe I'll be acceptable to God—maybe at last I'll receive His favor, sense His presence, experience His blessings.*

While letting God change negative behaviors is part of the goal (indeed, it's part of the plan), trying to pay our own way or submitting to performance-based faith is not. When we treat the Bible as a mere manual, we miss the Person behind the pages. What's more, God doesn't swap marbles. We don't earn heavenly tokens by checking off a daily list of sins avoided.

> If our sole motive to obey is to be blessed, we are simply attempting to manipulate God. The underlying assumption is: *I've been good enough . . . bless me.* It's true that we will reap what we sow. It's true that obedience keeps us within God's plan for our lives. But our decision to obey should never be based solely on God's rewarding us.[24]

We no longer see the Bible as "another religious text."

We've found that Jesus meets with us, and His Spirit illuminates us when we come humbly to engage His message. Max Lucado notes once more that "for the millions who have tested its claims and claimed its promises there is but one answer—the Bible is God's book and God's voice."[25]

We've also learned that wavering and double-mindedness are spiritual killers. If we don't believe what the Bible claims about itself, and view it as merely a historical document, how can we possibly know God and grow closer to Him?

Scripture is the foundation of every Christian belief. What we know about God and salvation we know because He has revealed it to us.

William Lyon Phelps, who taught at Yale for more than forty years, said: "I thoroughly believe in a university education . . . but I believe a knowledge of the Bible without a college course is more valuable than a college course without the Bible."[26] We couldn't agree more.

We no longer see the Bible as a talisman—a magic eight ball.

Ask a question, give a good shake, and the needed answer comes into view. That's how we once approached Scripture (maybe you've done this too). No wonder so many of us have been discouraged.

Yes, the Bible gives divine guidance. (God's Word *is* our authority). And yes, its pages provide plenty of answers to life's ultimate questions. But for the most part, God has given us big-picture directions to follow, not every single situation-specific solution. The Bible is more compass than road map.

Insisting on quick fixes and instant growth will keep us disillusioned. We must embrace patience and persistence, even amid spiritual struggle.

If the prophet Jeremiah were here, he'd probably identify with the turmoil many of us face today. He had plenty of his own, and at one point he was so discouraged he was tempted to doubt God's goodness. Yet as he consumed Scripture, God moved him through his pain and into a place of peace: "When your words came, I ate them; they were my joy and my heart's delight."[27]

God is ready to shape up the "spiritual loser" inside each of us, and He'll continue doing this until that day when we're with Him face-to-face. On *this* side of heaven, He's showing us how—step-by-step—to let go of what's been holding us down or tripping us up—fear, pride, bitterness, worry, past failures, old habits . . . *anything* that hinders. We're building the courage to surrender *this moment* to Christ. You can do exactly the same.

In the next chapter, we'll look at how Jesus Christ calls us to live: radically, selflessly—*biblically.*

How the Bible Is Organized

A library of sixty-six books, bound into a single volume, divided into two primary collections:

The Old Testament The first thirty-nine books reveal basics about life and creation, God's commitment to us, prophecies of Messiah, and why we need Christ: Rebellion against our Creator (sin) has resulted in our separation from Him. The Old Testament is divided into:

The Pentateuch (Genesis to Deuteronomy)—the foundation of God's story; instructs us in His ways

The history books (Joshua to Esther)—chronicles humankind's rebellion and God's faithfulness

The poetry books (Job to the Song of Solomon)—God's magnificence, mystery, and majesty unfold

The major prophets (Isaiah to Daniel)—God's holiness; a foreshadowing of the good news revealed in Jesus

The minor prophets (Hosea to Malachi)—devastation caused by idolatry; awaiting Messiah's coming

The New Testament The last twenty-seven books (via ten different authors) begin with the four Gospels and include a record of the gospel's spread (Acts), letters to individuals and churches, and general letters. Revelation tells of Christ's final triumph and the fate of all humanity.

————○————

Research Reveals: Ongoing study reveals that emotional well-being, hope, and the fruit of the Spirit (as outlined in Galatians 5:22–23) thrive when we engage the Bible, not by reading other "religious works" or secondary sources.

Encouraging Nudge: The Bible is true and trustworthy; it has stood and will stand the test of time. God's Word will transform all who live His message.

Take a look at unstuck.gotandem.com for more practical ways to grow spiritually. Do this every day during your forty-five-day journey.

Spiritual
Stepping Stones

● **DAY 25**

> **Scripture to Remember:** John 1:1–5
> **Question to Consider:** How does God's Word expose darkness?

● **DAY 26**

> **Scripture to Remember:** Jeremiah 15:1–21
> **Question to Consider:** How can Scripture quench my spiritual thirst?

● **DAY 27**

> **Scripture to Remember:** Luke 21:29–36
> **Question to Consider:** How do I overcome the "anxieties of life"?

ten

Moving Beyond "ME"

The flow of life surging and pulsing through me to refresh this weary old world must be from God Himself. It must be the continuous outpouring of His Presence by His Spirit. . . . Any person naïve enough, arrogant enough, stupid enough to believe that it is his or her own charm, charisma, or capabilities that change and enliven others, lives in utter self-delusion.[1]

—W. Phillip Keller

The words cut deep.

I (Arnie) had opened my Bible to 2 Timothy, which Paul wrote during particularly difficult times for the early church. Seeking some much-needed encouragement, I was expecting a pep talk and a warm, fuzzy hug.

Instead I felt the sting of a slap:

Don't be naïve. There are difficult times ahead. As the end approaches, people are going to be self-absorbed, money-hungry, self-promoting, stuck-up, profane, contemptuous of parents, crude, coarse, dog-eat-dog, unbending, slanderers, impulsively wild, savage, cynical, treacherous, ruthless, bloated windbags, addicted to lust, and allergic to God. They'll make a show of religion, but behind the scenes they're animals. Stay clear of these people.[2]

Had I been one of those bloated windbags?

My life had been calm and comfortable compared to Paul's; comfort and the Christian faith don't exactly go together. As I dug deep into his letter, I saw that life in Christ doesn't instantly eradicate problems. It's no "Exercise Just Eight Minutes a Day and Still Get All the Results You Want" plan.

Following Jesus is a long and difficult trek that can take us through some hostile territory. We get weary and messy along the way. The ground gets rocky; the hills get steep. Though Paul didn't see many pretty rainbows or cushy meadows, this Christ-follower remained steadfast. He stayed true to the One he was following, true to his mission of lighting up the darkness.

When Jesus says, "Come, follow Me," everything changes: our identities, our motives, how we handle adversity, how we relate to others. We finally get a clue that the center of the universe is not *ME*!

At least, that's how it's supposed to be.

What was missing from my life? How could I be more like Paul?

I turned my eyes to another Christ-follower. Todd Huston, a mountain climber with a disability, had a story that put everything in perspective for me.

Todd Huston swallowed hard. Today the obstacle he faced was Mount McKinley, the highest point in North America. Yesterday, it'd been learning to live with a disability.

170

If he reached the summit, he'd rank among the few elite climbers to conquer this giant. Even more impressive, he'd have done it on a prosthetic leg, which would make him king of an even bigger mountain.

After resting at a ridgetop, he continued his ascent up an extremely icy slope known as Pig Hill. Reinforcing his fears was everything he'd heard about the killer climb—crevasses, glaciers, sheer ice walls, violent storms, plummeting temperatures, whiteouts. This one would determine his fate, pushing him beyond anything he'd imagined during months of intense training. This wicked wall threatened to break him.

The rest is easy, he said silently. *Get past Pig Hill. The rest is easy.*

Yet with each step a fresh fury of pain exploded in his boot and seared the end of his stump. This most grueling climb was taking its toll on his body. His lungs threatened to burst with every breath. His heartbeat drummed and throbbed against his temples.

He was on the verge of surrender when his climbing partner pointed and yelled: "There it is—the summit!"

Todd gazed in awe. That pinnacle looked unconquerable. *We still have to go that much farther?*

But from Pig Hill it *was* an easy trek. Whether it was the gradual ascent or the adrenaline subduing his excitement, he maintained a steady pace along the ridge at twenty thousand feet.

Todd accelerated his pace and lunged the last few feet. His eyes caught sight of flags left by previous victors.

"Thank God!" he shouted. His voice filled every crevasse and canyon in Denali National Park.

After the expedition, he explained to a reporter: "I see myself as a representative of the forty-three million Americans who, on any given day, are struggling against a major illness, a disability, or any other health-related challenge." He went on to describe difficulties that wouldn't show up on any X ray—divorce, death of a loved one, overcoming addiction.

Todd Huston's physical issues had begun at fourteen, when a waterskiing accident severed his right leg. Amazingly, doctors saved and reattached the limb. But several weeks later, infection set in, and finally, after enduring twenty-eight surgeries and ongoing, agonizing physical therapy, this young man from Tulsa had to face the possibility of losing his leg. He said:

> I tried to hide my physical scars from my friends. I seldom swam, and I used humor to hide the mental scars. But what hurt most was not being able to play football. That sport had been my life. As a middle linebacker during seventh and eighth grade, I held the record at Byrd Junior High for the most tackles.

Questions about God and his relationship with Jesus swirled around his head. One day, while sitting in a park beneath a tree, he opened his Bible and began reading the Psalms. Then, he struggled to his feet and looked through the branches and leaves into the sky. "Lord, I'm yours," he prayed aloud.

Todd knew it was time to have a healthy body too. Having his right leg amputated just below his knee was the only solution. A gentle rush of God's power filled him with peace and the knowledge that Jesus would see him through the challenges ahead. But never in his wildest dreams did Todd imagine he'd one day stand on North America's apex.

> I had climbed my mountains and seen the other side. I had dodged thunderstorms, battled blizzards, endured incredible

pain, and faced my fears through faith in God. I had gained a deeper experience with Him. Time after time, when it seemed the expedition was doomed, He smoothed the way. Time after time, when my body hurt so badly that I thought I couldn't take another step, He infused me with the strength to continue. Time after time, He was there. Now I know He always will be.[3]

The "ME" I'd Been

Todd Huston was a true inspiration. What was holding *me* back?

Labels—that's what.

Labels, mixed with luxurious comfort and with mixed-up priorities.

I'd come to realize that I, that we, slap labels on everything. Not just our food, clothes, and cars either, on ourselves and others as well.

I jump into social mode when in a room filled with mingling people shaking hands and making small talk. There's a lot of eye contact and big smiles. Next thing I know, I'm exclaiming how good the cream puffs are. Self-marketing through sound-bite swapping, I exchange names (and, in turn, state my job, marital status, number of kids at which grade levels and which schools, neighborhood, church, and last, what brought me to this event).

Around the five-minute mark, someone new walks up, we rotate to another new face, and the intros start over. There's laughter and more smiles as we all size each other up. After a couple of hours, I find I'm reviewing my performance on the drive home. *Did they like me? Do I fit in? Should I really follow up on any of the dinner invites or on the playdate ideas for the kids? Or were they just being nice? Should I introduce myself, as a writer or as an author? How long would it take to learn to play golf—do they all play golf?*

Overall it went well. I was friendly and interesting. I didn't exaggerate or embellish. But the five-minute-cocktail-version of me—is that really *me*?

I've invested so much time in preparing for my future. I'm happily married, have wonderful children, continue to succeed at work, and manage my money wisely. *Is "Christian" just another achievement in my life? Isn't there supposed to be more?*

What God Says About "ME"

All of you, be like-minded, be sympathetic, love one another, be compassionate and humble.[4]

"Love the Lord your God with all your heart and with all your soul and with all your mind." This is the first and greatest commandment. And the second is like it: "Love your neighbor as yourself." All the Law and the Prophets hang on these two commandments.[5]

Feed my lambs.[6]

This is how God showed his love among us: He sent his one and only Son into the world that we might live through him. This is love: not that we loved God, but that he loved us and sent his Son as an atoning sacrifice for our sins.[7]

What would God's five-minute-cocktail-version-of-me be like?

Perhaps this is something like what He'd emphasize: *my child, forgiven, my hands and feet, saved, misguided, clean, my helper,* and so on. Not at all like how I identify and present myself. God knows the real me, not just the one I promote while trying to eat food bits off toothpicks. I can't help but wonder what it would be like to see myself as God does.

How would it change my daily life? What would happen if I stopped expending so much energy on *my* future and increasingly saw reality through *His* eyes?

While I'm not sure I even know how to start, I see that I'm surrounded by needy people every day. I drive past the City Mission on my way to work. I see folks lined up in hopes of a warm meal. There are young children walking alone to school without hat or gloves. The bad news about the most recent famine, war, refugee situation, and natural disaster is so prevalent and so nonstop that I've become numb to the hurt, the need, and the cries for help.

How can I start being the man God sees?

Remember Theresa, the young woman who went from rules to relationship?[8] She's well into a successful medical career, yet her profession doesn't define her. Through prayer and Bible engagement, she began to sense the Lord calling her to something more and moving her to another level of relationship with Him.

Theresa would have fit right in serving alongside the apostle Paul—he'd have been proud of her. Below she shares how God is working in her life today.

The "ME" We're Called to Be

Now a board-certified physician assistant for thirty years, I've been privileged to work with amazing medical teams in Africa and Asia. Poverty's toll on the world, especially on the children, has been unimaginable at times. I've seen families dig holes in the ground to have a place for their children to sleep. An estimated twelve thousand people (two-thirds of them in sub-Saharan Africa) die daily from HIV/ AIDS, tuberculosis, or malaria. At this moment, in Ethiopia (one of the countries I've worked in most), 2.2 million live with HIV/AIDS.

I will never forget my first trip there. I saw countless emaciated children infected with the disease that's killing entire nations. They were in the arms of mothers with blank, forlorn looks; sometimes tears would fill their eyes as they begged us to heal their children. My heart broke again and again as I held their children and gently shook my head, explaining that I had no medicines to help. It seemed hopeless.

In the world's second poorest country, most people have no coat and wear everything they own in winter to stay warm. The average family makes about $200 a year (not even sixty cents a day) and can't afford milk or meat for the children. Even those who have food are malnourished; children have difficulty learning without the vitamins and nutrition needed for their brains—if they get to go to school at all.

In the most impoverished countries, mothers risk their lives giving birth. Millions of children die each year from treatable, preventable causes like diarrhea. Right now, overall, the number of children out of school exceeds the population of primary-school-aged children on the entire continents of Europe and North America combined.

Nearly 900 million people on the globe have no access to clean water; 2.6 billion are without adequate sanitation. In rural Rwanda, children or their parents must walk two hours each way for clean water to take care of the family's daily needs. Even that water, filled with parasites and germs, must be boiled for drinking. The energy spent in the endeavor often keeps carriers from being able to intake sufficient calories—their malnourishment is compounded with dehydration.

I've worked extensively in the surgical disciplines, and I enjoy it. There's something so satisfying about being able to examine and diagnose a specific condition, then go cut it out or fix it. "Healed!" we exclaim over our patients' sleeping bodies in the recovery room.

The pride that can come with this kind of knowledge and power, though, sometimes cripples its possessor. And until I went to India, I didn't realize I was crippled—crippled like so many of my little patients beyond human cure.

I'm a fix-it girl. Have a problem? Tell me what it is; I'll unravel it, dissect it, get to the bottom of it, or come up with a solution. I was told from a young age I could do anything I set my mind to. I grew up believing that, and I still do. Nothing is impossible.

But in Ghana, or Vietnam, or Ethiopia, or most recently in India, I've sat with limp hands, powerless to heal children brought to me.

Somewhere in my mind I hear the enemy laughing at the helplessness I feel in those moments when there's nothing I can do. He laughs at me when I'm frail and weak, taunting me with hopelessness. Every day it's war in my little exam room, and I struggle.

I'm sure my colleagues have seen this in me. They probably have not understood the origin of my frustration, but they've been on the receiving end of it . . . and they have handled me with love and grace and mercy. I also know that they've prayed for me.

And in Manipur, India, something changed inside. God broke through my blindness and brought light. There was a victory for which I hadn't even known to ask.

For two straight days, a Bnei Menashe mother—her face has always remained in my mind—sat before me on a little plastic chair. Her little boy was very sick with a fever, and because we'd run out of children's Ibuprofen we gave another medicine and had him return for a recheck the next day. But he also had cerebral palsy. I could only treat his fever and help to educate his weary mom to see that it probably was helping more than hurting him.

I could not cure his CP. The helper was helpless.

177

Now, I don't mind being given this responsibility. I've been doing it for years in America, where there's abundance and resources and help. But on the mission field, where we're meant to give more than people are used to receiving, the powerlessness I feel can be bitter. Tears come; my heart breaks every single day. Wheels start turning in my head, too many wheels, and I start pondering, "If only . . ."

If only we had a therapist with us . . . if only we had a pediatric surgeon . . . if only I had funds for this operation . . . if only . . . if only . . .

There I was again, on the other side of the world with the mother of a sick child sitting in front of me for the second day. I knew there was nothing I could do. When my moment of fear returned, God spoke: "Teach her," He said, "then hand him to Me."

There was a visual image in my mind of Abraham laying Isaac on the altar. In an instant, a God-moment, I realized that all these years I'd been trying to save Isaac from the altar of sacrifice when it was God's work to redeem. He wanted me to take the child in my arms, bless him, and offer him up. And then let it go. So this is what I did.

Bending down, I gently told the mother that while I had no power to heal her son or make his mind and body strong, Yeshua (Jesus) loves him and wanted to bless him. I asked her permission to pray a blessing over her boy. I took him in my lap and began to pray; I spoke health and strength over his mind and body. I asked God for blessings on the whole family in Jesus' name, blessings of provision and strength.

After the prayer, tears were in the mother's eyes. Her son now was laid on the altar of God. I believe with all my heart that He can and will strengthen this little boy. It truly would be a miracle if we return next year to find him speaking and growing and walking.

However, I've come to embrace that the results of faith are not up to me. They're all God's: "Suffer the little children to come unto me . . ." Sometimes, when they cannot run to Him themselves, we must carry them to His feet and release them into His capable arms. This was a true revelation for me, a "fixer," and for all the "fixing" I try to do in the field, I have realized, and I did perhaps for the first time in India, that in the process, God is "fixing" me.

The world is hungry: starving for food, crying out for provision, longing for shelter . . . desperately in need of life. They're oppressed by corrupt governments, and by principalities and powers that seek to steal, kill, and destroy. What are they entitled to? What are their rights?

I was compelled to consider the way I live my life in view of the gospel, with the whole world in my view! The purpose of educating ourselves about the rest of the world is to see that we're not its center—it doesn't revolve around us. This truth isn't meant to bring guilt but true enlightenment; not to make us feel overwhelmed, but concerned. We are the princes and princesses of God's kingdom. He calls us to rule and to reign with servant hearts, to lay down our lives . . . to be our brother's keeper.

I used to feel very overwhelmed. Fortunately I heard about and joined initiatives that can make a difference: the One Campaign, The Global Fund, (RED), and Christian organizations like Compassion International and World Vision, who are providing food, shelter, education, and medication to save lives all over the world. And of course the group I go with, though not as well-known, gives me the opportunity to share the gospel and medicine in many places.

The "ME" for All Eternity

It's a struggle to live what I (Arnie) believe. I'm a child of God, and I want to serve Him. I want Him to be pleased as I reach out to those around me with His love and compassion. But it sure would be easier to be the five-minute-cocktail-version-of-me. There seems to be a never-ending tension between what others want from me and what my Savior expects.

It's hard to consider others' needs and not obsess over my own amid my everyday hustle and bustle. Yet all around me are the homeless and the houseless; there's the pain of divorce, the chains of addiction, the fear of illness, the sting of death. I don't have to go far, much less travel halfway around the world, to push through my cocoon. Daily I'm challenged to step forth and invite God to speak in life's extraordinary ordinary moments.

I'm not the world's center—I'm God's hands and feet, right here in my own neighborhood, workplace, and church. I don't sign up for a ten-day mission trip and then think I'm ahead of the curve or have met my quota. Loving, caring, giving, serving: that's a lifestyle.

Christ *empowers* me to help my neighbor. God's loving presence is poured out to others through me. Everything we need is found in Him: "My God will meet all your needs according to the riches of his glory in Christ Jesus."[9]

What's your source—where do you go—for your empowerment? How do you become filled with God's love? *Go to, and remain in, His Word.*

It's easy to ask, "What's in it for *me*? I've worked hard—I deserve some rest, comfort, situational security. You don't know what my past was like, what I've endured and survived." But staying stuck in the primacy of our own entitlement and emphasizing past achievements or failures simply keeps our eyes on *us*. The more we make our goals our identity, and the more we prize our own circumstances, the more self-centered we become. God can set us free to live as the real us, by His definition: saved, forgiven, His child, His hands and feet. . . .

We find that freedom in intimacy with Him. What are we waiting for?

———◉———

In Part Three we'll get even more personal and practical. We'll show you how to *live* Powered by Four and *grow* your faith. We'll start with an honest discussion about God, as it's impossible to get unstuck spiritually if we have wrong or incomplete perceptions of who He is and how He wants us to live.

———◉———

Research Reveals: We lose the day spiritually . . .

1. When we don't engage God
2. When we don't engage Scripture
3. When we stay in a "notional relationship"
4. When we replace intimacy with ritual
5. When we get comfortable with selfishness, wrong thinking, and soul-harming behaviors

Encouraging Nudge: Accepting being mired in the past keeps my eyes frozen on *me*. But life wasn't created with *me* at reality's center, and it won't be sustained that way either. As I reflect on and relate to the person of Jesus, I'm able to turn from my struggles and failures. *Today* is important to the Lord, so each day is a gift to fully engage with a thankful heart and an attitude of expectant hope.

Take a look at unstuck.gotandem.com for more practical ways to grow spiritually. Do this every day during your forty-five-day journey.

Spiritual
Stepping Stones

● **DAY 28**

Scripture to Remember: Ezekiel 36:24–38

Question to Consider: How does God enable my "human spirit" to do His will?

● **DAY 29**

Scripture to Remember: 2 Corinthians 5:1–10

Question to Consider: What must I do to live by faith, not by sight?

● **DAY 30**

Scripture to Remember: Ephesians 2:11–22

Question to Consider: Why are selflessness and unity with other believers two keys to knowing and doing God's will?

Engage, Untangle . . . Grow!

By the End of Part Three You'll Be Able to:

- Plot your own course toward a spiritual breakthrough
- Clarify God's purpose for your life
- Manage and keep in check your weaknesses, with Christ's help
- Engage the Bible's protective factor by "taking up your sword [God's Living Word] and shield [your faith in Jesus Christ]"
- Steer clear of shortcuts to spiritual growth

eleven

Regaining the Wonder

Why am I afraid to dance, I who love music and rhythm and grace and song and laughter? Why am I afraid to live, I who love life and the beauty of flesh and the living colors of the earth and sky and sea? Why am I afraid to love, I who love love?[1]

—Eugene O'Neill

We're ready for change.

No more fumbling around in a fog, no more running hard but never getting anywhere. We'll stop faking it, and we'll start surrendering our weakness.

We know we can't do it by ourselves, but we don't have to. We know who to lean into.

We're ready for the things we need most: real purpose, real life . . . real faith.

Remember the spiritual menace we talked about earlier? Not temptation, but the one before that: our busy lives—our "staying busy being busy."

Medical doctors and psychologists tell us that merely "existing" on a treadmill of stress and busyness is unhealthy (physically *and* spiritually). We hear this all the time; we know it's true, so why do we do nothing about it?

Busyness steals away the wonder of faith, of salvation, of eternity. It stalls our walk and stunts our growth. When we keep running crazy but going nowhere, the enemy stands a greater chance of wreaking havoc on our lives.

After years of spinning wheels, something radical happened to Tiffany: She met Jesus with her *heart* and truly began to *live*, to grow spiritually. And this was no mountaintop encounter that evaporated when life got tough again. Tiffany figured out where to turn for answers when her faith was stuck.

Listen as this young wife and mother shares her story in her own words.

Exhausted—again. No different from any other random day. The alarm began its annoying buzz at 6:30; I started my morning stretch routine to shut it up. Every nine minutes my arm snuck out from under warm covers to hit my clock—which is also my cell phone.

Of course it is. Why would I sleep more than three feet from my lifeline? I need something to do at 2:34 a.m. when I'm wide awake. I can return emails, check the weather, send a birthday text, add to my shopping list, take notes for the novel I've been working on for years, review my prayer list, search for my dream vacation, transfer money between accounts, even play a round of Mahjong. I usually stop when my wrists begin to exhibit my near-certain, near-future case of carpal tunnel.

If I'm still awake I can always get up and fold laundry or unload/reload the dishwasher. Usually I just lie there frustrated and sleepless till finally I get around to God. (My "prayer" usually begins with, "Why can't I sleep?")

But then I find myself recalling how amazing He is and how lucky I am.

After several minutes of praise and reflection, I fall into deep slumber. So I shouldn't be surprised that when I stretch out to hit Snooze I often find a more comfortable position. My body feels smooth and relaxed and . . . I leap to my feet suddenly, in sheer panic. How many times did I snooze? Not again!

I quickly delete tasks from my to-do list to have a chance of getting out the door in time. Microwave breakfast, throw on clean clothes (just folded three hours ago), turn the ringer on, swipe the snow off the car, race out for the day, throughout which I'll guzzle caffeine and gulp power foods as I multitask.

I send out detailed status reports at work. I hit the gym several times a week. I compare prices and find the best deal in town before I shop. I volunteer at church. I invest a lot of time and energy landscaping my yard. I go to lunch with friends. I get the oil changed every three thousand miles. I take the cats to the vet. When I've tried to slow down, I've just felt guilty.

Why would I do less than I'm capable of?

I work so hard trying to build the life I want—the one I feel I deserve from all the hard work. But lately I've been wondering if that's what I'm supposed to be working toward. Early morning conversations with God have been leading me to reexamine my goals. Could my life be different? Should it be? I know a believer's life is supposed to be better, but what does that mean?

As I look around, it seems I'm kind of like everyone else.

Warning: If you ask God for direction, He's going to give it to you. My short attention span was bouncing all over the place as I sat in traffic. I inched to the left as far as possible to see what was going on up the street. Out of luck and hemmed in by a six-inch median, I began to flip through radio channels.

Even crawling along at two miles an hour I wouldn't allow myself to text or check e-mail. And I'd already left a voicemail for everyone I know. So I thought maybe even a talk show would be better than nothing.

Through an array of preachers shouting over the airwaves, I found one who was soft-spoken; he was drawing his lesson to a close and sounded as though he was trying to hold back tears. I don't know his name or his program, but I remember his closing plea for all believers to read God's Word: "You want to know what it means to be a Christian? God wants you to know. He has given us His Word. It's His story . . . pick it up, blow off the dust, and read it! Read it every day. And then hold on, because you've just tapped in to God."

I stared in disbelief. The Bible. Why didn't I think of that? I'm a longtime believer and have read it but didn't even think of it when I began my search for direction. There it is—right in front of me. Actually, it's all around me. I have ten or more versions in all sizes and colors around my house.

I wasn't sure how to start. Should I go straight through? Start with the Gospels? Psalms are always inspirational. Do I really have to revisit Revelation? So I just jumped in, randomly opening it up and starting to read.

Soon I signed up for daily devotionals via e-mail. (Now I had a better reason for never setting down my phone.) They came with insight and, most important, Scripture references. I'd pull out my Bible and look them up, which sometimes would lead me to other related passages.

Next thing I knew, I'd worked my way through a handful of New Testament books. I shouldn't say work—I looked forward to time with God! This started working its way into my daily life.

I was able to offer a college student advice from that day's devotional. I began seeing others through God's eyes. I started taking donations to the local food bank and sponsoring a child overseas. I became friendlier. Early morning times of prayer became praise sessions. I began paying attention to evangelism. I found inspiration as I learned about recent-era martyrs. I began to find my place in the larger picture of Christian history, which helped me to feel connected to the stories and people in the Bible (who didn't get it right all the time either).

Yes, I was relieved I wasn't the only believer who messes up.

Yet inevitably I'd need to take a closer look at my own life. Why was I working so hard? Allowing myself to be worn out and preoccupied with all things me seemed crazy. I'd spent so many years pouring myself into self-promotion and self-preservation. My future was my goal, but it really wasn't God's. He wants my heart, my mind, my soul. He wants my energy. He wants my dreams to be His and for me to serve Him, whether right here in my own backyard or in a village on the other side of the world.

Honestly, I wasn't prepared for the reality of seeing through Christ's eyes. This was hard, sweet, hopeful, and sometimes tear-filled. The busyness of constant multitasking had numbed my heart to hunger cries of defenseless children, to persecution of fellow believers, to numerous injustices against the innocent.

Jesus has called me to care: "I was hungry and you gave me something to eat, I was thirsty and you gave me something to drink, I was a stranger and you invited me in, I needed clothes and you clothed me, I was sick and you looked after me, I was in prison and you came to visit me."[2]

Jesus has called me to surrender: "Whoever wants to be my disciple must deny themselves and take up their cross and follow me. For whoever wants to save their life will lose it, but whoever loses their life for me will find it. What good will it be for someone to gain the whole world, yet forfeit their soul? Or what can anyone give in exchange for their soul?"[3]

Simply put, Jesus has called me to GET UP, GO, and GROW. And I now have a clear idea of the first steps He wants me to take.

Embrace the Son

The Son is the radiance of God's glory and the exact representation of his being, sustaining all things by his powerful word.[4]

Embrace the Journey

Here's what I want you to do, God helping you: Take your everyday, ordinary life—your sleeping, eating, going-to-work, and walking-around life—and place it before God as an offering. Embracing what God does for you is the best thing you can do for him. Don't become so well-adjusted to your culture that you fit into it without even thinking. Instead, fix your attention on God. You'll be changed from the inside out. Readily recognize what he wants from you, and quickly respond to it. Unlike the culture around you, always dragging you down to its level of immaturity, God brings the best out of you, develops well-formed maturity in you.[5]

Embrace the Wonder

Our Father in heaven,
hallowed be your name,
your kingdom come,
your will be done
on earth as it is in heaven.

Give us today our daily bread.

And forgive us our debts,

    as we also have forgiven our debtors.

And lead us not into temptation,

    but deliver us from the evil one.[6]

Learning to Walk Again

Jesus may take us to some uncomfortable places and call us to have a heart for other messy people. Not only is it not easy seeing life through Christ's eyes, it also can feel downright scary.

What is God asking me to face . . . to overcome in my own life? What's He calling me to say . . . to do in the lives of others? I don't feel ready. It seems like He wants me to take on the impossible.

That's how God operates!

When we surrender our weakness, His strength takes over, and He makes a way. That's why we simply can't remain worn out and directionless. We must take our eyes off dead things and start living again—or for the first time.

Living means *caring*; *caring* means *growing*.

Let's learn to walk. As we engage the Bible and take steps toward spiritual growth, it's important that we put away shortsightedness and indifference and take to heart how Christ intended for us to use God's Word. Remember Dr. Kroll's words? "By stopping to 'taste' the Bible—really taking it in and savoring it—we learn to trust God in a whole new way."[7]

Let's taste some key insights on Matthew 6:9–13 (known as the Lord's Prayer), a passage Tiffany mentioned. There are important themes needing our attention. If we quickly whip through what Jesus says, we could miss out on what He wants us to hear. The themes are:

1. God is
2. Where God is
3. What God is like
4. How God wants us to live
5. How God wants us to find our destiny

Wrong or incomplete perceptions about these will hinder our connection with God. Grasping the essential elements Jesus wants us to capture is foundational to getting unstuck spiritually. And, if we're not growing spiritually, we're likely losing the battle.

Where's this leading us? Not so much a place as a state of mind: *wonder.*

In this passage (and in others), Jesus begins with the perspective of childlike wonder because of how much we need it while navigating through this difficult and complicated life. Wonder leads us to trust in something bigger than ourselves; it brings about healthy awe and inspires an appropriate gratefulness; it's a path to worship, the way to approach our heavenly Father.

Lessons From a Child's Eye

When do children tend to lose their wonder of the world around them?

When does a young boy realize his dad actually *didn't* hang the moon and really *can't* beat up any other dad with one hand tied behind his back?

When does a little girl come to perceive she's not a little princess and feel that she's just another body trying to compete with countless others for the attention she so desperately craves?

These are sad changes in young hearts and minds. The truth is, everyone grows up and loses the wonder at some point. It happens to children; it happens in our relationships; it happens in our walk with God.

There was a time in my (Arnie's) life when the wonder of God began to fade. He became a list of *can'ts*, a guy to learn about on boring Sundays. I'd completely lost any notion of God's creative power and of heaven's splendor.

In short, God wasn't anyone I really *desired* relationship with. I'd lost my heart for the wonder of His love for me, His care for me, His promises that ensured I could completely trust His goodness as a loving Father.

Any relationship begins when we acquire a heart to pursue. Of course, this is true especially when it comes to the opposite sex. Who can't remember the first time you fell in love and experienced the wonder of romance?

This also is true of friendship, when the wonder of that someone "who understands and accepts me for who I am" suddenly crystallizes. And how about parenting—is there anything more wonder-filled than a newborn in your arms during the first months? Something deep within us experiences *wonder* and says, "I need this more than life itself."

Then, as you've likely experienced, with few exceptions, the wonder fades. When the wonder becomes a memory we swap for comfortable routines, for behavior that seems right, for knowledge—good things, but simply not equivalent to the passion that true wonder can bring.

Our sense of wonder about God as He's found throughout the Bible doesn't last forever on its own energy. The wonder of discovering His story and its pervasive interconnection with our own can be awe-inspiring during those first years as a believer. As time marches on, as we read and reread, our ability to take in all the magnificence can seem lost and even irretrievable.

Cutting Ourselves Some Slack

The Lord walked in Eden with Adam and Eve, and *they* didn't get it right either. They knew firsthand the wonder of face-to-face encounters with God—hearing His voice, feeling His touch on their shoulder. They literally, daily, hung out with God.

And consider this: That sacred place made perfect relationships possible. It was here that God created Eve from Adam's body[8] and spoke intimately and directly with His children.[9] They could eat freely from a tree whose fruit gave them endless life. As far as we can determine, Adam and Eve could have lived eternally in wonder there had they not done the one and only thing God warned them not to do.

Eden, then, was vastly different from our world today—there was no sorrow, no strife, no death, and no separation from God. So Adam and Eve, when they fell, had a clear knowledge of the wonder they'd lost. Their sense of being apart from God must have filled their every thought and dream.

What did they call their Creator afterward? Did His name change from *Teacher* to *Judge*? Maybe *Friend* changed to *Almighty*? I'm sure their vantage of and perspective toward their God changed as their circumstances changed.

Sound familiar?

In all the millennia since, God could potentially become seen as more and more distant with each successive century . . . especially if we ignore the entirety of His revelation to us as we seek to discover His character. The question "What is God like?" is always relevant.

God's nature and character are described in so many ways—*holy, compassionate, merciful, gracious, loving, faithful* (to name just a few). And if there's one essential trait all of humanity can celebrate, it's probably *giving*. We have life only because God has created us by an exercise of His will. We can receive salvation only because He has willed to grant it.

God's heart never stops giving. It's because of His nature that we're able to approach Him. "Your voice matters in heaven," says Max Lucado. "He takes you very seriously. When you enter His presence, He turns to you to hear your voice. No need to fear that you will be ignored."[10]

Father, Alpha, Omega, Shepherd, Yahweh, Creator—all these names (and many more) can get a little confusing. Why so many? Is this just another "religious disagreement" issue? Can't we come up with one to encompass them all? I remember feeling a bit overwhelmed the first time I pondered these things. A few years and some experiences later, though, I not only get why so many names are attributed to God, I'm also very thankful for them. It's another facet of reality that fills me with wonder. I have called out to my Lord using every one of these names (and others).

How about you? When you think of God, what images come to mind? A scowling, gavel-banging judge? An unapproachable burning bush? Simply a spirit? A loving father? A bearded Middle Eastern man with dirty sandals and sun-weathered skin?

How do your daily circumstances filter your perception of the Almighty? And how will your view of God be impacted as you immerse yourself in His Word?

The Jesus I Know

Approximately seven billion humans are on the earth right now. Consider how many already have lived and how many more are on the way—it's a lot of people! *Every single one* has been handcrafted by God himself—each with a personality, experiences, and dreams. And each one changes every day as we live. This is how God made us, and it's also how He relates to us. We have so many names for Him because our need for Him is so great; He is everything to us, even if we don't yet know it.

All of His names are to be "hallowed,"[11] because He is.

God is the Shepherd who guides, the Lord who provides, the Lord of peace during life's trials, the Physician who heals the sick, the Banner that guides the soldier.[12]

He is Alpha and Omega, "the beginning and the end."

He is Immanuel, "God with us."

He is our Father.

He is holy.

He is love.[13]

The God in whom you trust is the infinite Creator who has always been and always will be—who spoke the universe into being by the power of His Word. He told Moses, "I am who I am" (self-existent; ever present). Truly, there is only one; He is the sovereign Lord, the God of Scripture, who acts in His creation and involves himself intimately in our lives.[14]

In *Knowing God*, J. I. Packer describes five basic truths about Him:

- *God has spoken to humankind*—and the Bible is His Word, given to teach us about salvation and to make us wise in His ways.
- *God is Lord and King over His world*—He rules all things for His own glory, displaying His perfection in all that He does, in order that people and angels may worship and adore Him.

- *God is our Savior*—active in sovereign love through the Lord Jesus Christ to rescue believers from the guilt and power of sin, to adopt them as His children and to bless them accordingly.
- *God is triune*—within the Godhead are three persons: Father, Son, and Holy Spirit; all three act together in the work of salvation, the Father purposing, the Son securing, and the Spirit applying redemption.
- *Godliness means responding to God's revelation*—in trust and obedience, faith and worship, prayer and praise, submission and service. Life must be seen and lived in the light of God's Word. This, and nothing else, is true religion.[15]

Following the Son

Remember that "the Son is the radiance of God's glory and the exact representation of his being, sustaining all things by his powerful word."[16] He said, "If you've seen me, you've seen the Father."[17] The straightforward answer to "What is God's character like?" is *Jesus*.

When I began to follow my own way in my early twenties, I'd come to some selfish and immature conclusions about the life of faith. I reasoned that since I couldn't live purely in my actions, I wouldn't try. When I came to the end of myself, more than a quarter century later, I started to look deeper and found that God doesn't mete out attention or affection via debits and credits; He's an unconditional lover of anyone who humbly acknowledges sin and genuinely realizes a need for the Savior.

If we humbly look to Him and ask that He "have mercy on me, a sinner,"[18] He's delighted to oblige. We cannot fathom or grasp His love, but He forgives our sin through Jesus Christ

197

and brings us back into fellowship with Him. Abandoning His wayward children is unthinkable to God, the father of every prodigal son and daughter. There's something awe-inspiringly ultimate about the simplicity of His unceasing, boundless love for us.

What of heaven, the third major theme to which Jesus points us? Though a cursory look in a short chapter doesn't do it justice, we must note that He reminds us of God's dwelling for a reason: Focusing on heaven keeps the mystery and wonder of *all that He is* at the forefront of our minds.

God knew we needed at least one aspect of His kingdom that we couldn't figure out. We know much of His character, we know much about His plan, but we only have human descriptions of the eternal wonders awaiting us. Heaven is so unimaginably wondrous that our terms scarcely can illustrate its splendor. Its mysteries are a gift to be opened at the time only God knows.

Heaven will be the homecoming at which we finally see what the Lover of our souls has designed for our everlasting life with Him.

It will be *WONDER-FULL.*

Putting It All Together: Engage, Untangle . . . Grow!

In the words of Eugene O'Neill, let's "dance, laugh, live . . . love."[19]

And *grow.*

Engage the Bible daily, chew on each word, savor the very personal messages to you . . . meet God there. He has given us what we need to know about our faith walk with Him. Scripture compels me daily to desire a renewed passion to learn everything I can about Him. Yes, sometimes passages don't make sense until they all fit together. That's why it's so essential to keep engaging and allowing God to speak through them. Let *Him* put the parts together. Just keep walking, seeking, and pursuing.

Once again, Christ-followers who are thriving have clued in to a secret: life in Jesus. True Christianity isn't a religion but a *relationship,* an intimate, minute-by-minute walk with a Person. With this distinction driving their hearts and minds, they've found their place within the body. They try to avoid wasting time on pursuits that counter God's will. They're guided by (1) a clear vision of who Christ is, (2) a vital connection with Him, and (3) the keys to "putting off" or "putting away" old-life characteristics and "putting on" characteristics of our new life.

Further, many Christ-followers seek to zero in on how God wants them to live and what He wants them to undertake.[20] They've identified their talents and are using them toward the work that expresses them best. As a result, they experience reduced stress, increased balance, and high satisfaction.

Are these your desires as well? If so, plot a course by taking these steps.

First Step: *Focus Your Vision*

Three critical questions to ask yourself:

What is my perception of God?

What things are blocking a spiritual breakthrough in my life?

How can I work through them to get my faith moving again?

After taking some time to ponder, go to www.unstuck .gotandem.com for ideas on how to spark a breakthrough.

You can do a spiritual-growth assessment and receive a customized plan for getting growing. (Those who bought this book can receive this service *free* for forty-five days.)

A close relationship with Jesus is the foundation. Is God directing your steps? If so, you're going the right way: "Commit to the Lord whatever you do, and he will establish your plans."[21] But your plans have no strength if they're not from Him.

The Holy Spirit deals with each person in a personal and intimate way, convicting, directing, and influencing. You can literally walk in His presence if you stay engaged through Bible engagement, prayer, and connection with other believers.

Jesus communicates! The Lord answers your questions and guides your steps through Scripture, prayer time, circumstances, even the counsel of others. It's smart to consult with wise Christians and seriously consider their advice as you plot your course.

Peace is a sign of spiritual awareness. It also is often a good indication of being on the right track. And as you grow closer and closer to Christ, your instincts will become more sensitive to His influence. Your mind and spirit will become more in tune to God, and you'll hear Him more and more clearly, just as with any good friend.

Second Step: *Dare to Dream*

Take a look at your spiritual gifts and life dreams. Do some serious soul-searching and think about your interests, desires, and the kinds of things you'd like to pursue. In the process:

- Consider the gifts and talents God has given you. Ask Him to reveal what His good, pleasing, and perfect will looks like for you.[22]

- Share your dreams. Talk with a family member or close Christian friend. The input of those who know your aspirations can be of value in seeking the life pursuit that will best shape the real you.

Third Step: *Pinpoint Your Personality*

I'm often described as (circle only one pair of terms):

Mechanically Minded/Technical
Inventive/A Problem-Solver
Creative/Artistic
An Outdoor Enthusiast/Adventurous
Athletic/Competitive
Scientific/Mathematical
Investigative/A Fact-Finder
Legal-Minded/Detail-Oriented
A People Person/A Communicator
A Planner/An Organizer

Fourth Step: *Double-Check Your Wiring*

Zero in on how you grow spiritually. Respond to the following.

Means through which I grow best include:

Intensive Bible Study
Corporate Worship
Sermons and Inspiring Messages
Technology (e.g., Online Bible Studies/Discussion Groups)
Music and Art

Experiential Methods (e.g., Teaching and Serving)
Time Alone in Deep Reflection and Meditation

Other things that help me grow include:

1.
2.
3.

Things that block growth in me include:

1.
2.
3.

My top ten sources of inspiration include (list people, books, service projects, movies, places/environments, journeys, talks, mission trips, etc.):

1.
2.
3.
4.
5.
6.
7.
8.
9.
10.

My strengths include:

_____

_____

My weaknesses include:

_____

_____

I would describe my faith as notional because/relational because (choose one and explain):

_____

_____

What I'd love to tell someone but don't because I'm afraid to speak up is (only write it down if you want to):

_____

_____

Key ways in which I'm going to nurture a relational faith include (write your top five thoughts/ideas, perhaps based on what you've read):

1.
2.
3.
4.
5.

Fifth Step: *Set Some Spiritual-Growth Goals*

Goals for a thriving spiritual life have similarities to goals in athletics or training. You strive to attain them. There's joy in achieving them. You long to execute them again. Don't be afraid to set some goals for your life.

Such a goal is concrete, measurable, and attainable.

A concrete goal is one you can define clearly by putting it into words.

An intention "to be a good Christian" is vague and not very tangible. But "to pick up a Bible-engagement tool and begin using it consistently," for instance, is solid. Goals are best written down.

A measurable goal is one that allows you to see your progress.

"Know Scripture from cover to cover" is tough to measure. But "read the New Testament this summer," for example, allows you to mark your progression with the equivalent of a bookmark (or the ribbon marker in your Bible).

An attainable goal is one that can reasonably be completed.

"Lead the world to Christ" is both concrete and measurable but hardly attainable. "Introduce three people to Jesus this year" meets all three criteria.

Sixth Step: *Seek God*

This is a key in getting your goals and dreams into motion. Take an afternoon, a weekend, or an hour a day for a month—whatever you need—and chew on some of the "Spiritual Stepping Stones" verses throughout this book. Remember to engage the Bible—receive it, reflect on it, and respond to it. Above all, listen to God. Focus on His voice and His direction for you.

Next, begin writing some concrete, measurable, attainable goals for your spiritual life. Write them out and/or type them up. You'll want a clean copy to review and rehash on occasion. Setting growth goals isn't a one-time event.

---◉---

In the next chapter, we'll look at how you can manage your temptations and weaknesses, with Christ's help, and keep them in check.

———◉———

Research Reveals: Bible disengagement leaves believers ignorant of basic scriptural truths, vulnerable to false teachings, spiritually immature, and reflecting not on the one true God but on a fantasy-based image.

Encouraging Nudge: "Unto us a child is born, unto us a son is given . . . and his name shall be called Wonderful."[23] Even now He's working in ways just as amazing as when He created heaven and earth. Your challenge in the days ahead: Endeavor to get the full picture of God, as He has revealed himself, and be drawn to Him, amazed by Him—*with new awe and new wonder.*

Take a look at unstuck.gotandem.com for more practical ways to grow spiritually. Do this every day during your forty-five-day journey.

Spiritual
Stepping Stones

● DAY 31

Scripture to Remember: Colossians 1:15–20

Question to Consider: Do I have a wrong or incomplete perception of who God is? (What must I change? How will I change?)

DAY 32

Scripture to Remember: Hebrews 1:1–4

Question to Consider: I refer to Jesus as my Lord and Savior, and I call myself a Christ-follower. How will my walk with Him be different as I labor to get unstuck and to begin growing again?

DAY 33

Scripture to Remember: Revelation 1:4–8

Question to Consider: Am I ready to let Jesus Christ be the foundation of my life? Am I ready to live for *Him*—not just for myself?

twelve

Managing the "Dark Side"

———

I am a strange creature with two opposing minds in one body. Two distinct life forces in me keep trying to control my actions. . . . I can't explain why I am such a dual person when it comes to right and wrong. The evil that I hate is always present in me. The good and moral desires are there too, keeping my mind in constant turmoil.[1]

—David Wilkerson

There's this guy in Seattle who sings everywhere—coffeehouses, bars, music festivals, churches—anywhere he can draw a crowd. His voice has that gritty edge, and his songs churn up all kinds of emotions in those who listen. They make you think. Even cry.

His beat-up twelve-string guitar, covered with surfing stickers, duct tape, and "graffiti" (notes and doodles from friends, autographs), looks like a yard-sale reject. Amazingly, he somehow coaxes beauty out of something so ugly.

This guy is talented, yet—like his guitar—his life is pretty messy.

It started out that way.

His mom and dad abandoned him when he was a small boy, pawning him off on his grandparents. Not even in kindergarten, barely able to write his name, and already his young heart was torn and bruised. He started believing he was so unlovable, so flawed, that his parents couldn't stand to be around him. When they ended up divorcing, he blamed himself for that too. A toxic mix of shame, self-loathing, and rage began gurgling and bubbling inside.

Things gradually and increasingly got messier; he abused alcohol and other drugs during his teen years. As a young man he plunged deep into Rasta, searching for meaning but ending up more confused (not to mention usually sky-high). He hit rock bottom at twenty-four and spent time behind bars for using and dealing drugs.

And then he met Jesus.

And then everything began to fall into place . . . right? He did a "Christian 180" and now lives each moment in light of the fact that he's living forever.

Not exactly.

Despite ten years of "trying to get it right," his life is still pretty messy.

He reads his Bible, he prays, he devours every spiritual growth book he can find, he serves in church, he hangs out with Christ-following friends—he does all kinds of "Christian things" believers are supposed to do, yet he still slips on life's messes and falls flat on his face.

In fact, he's even dealing with new twists to old problems: *abandonment* (this time by his wife), *divorce* (this time his own), *imprisonment* (this time his emotions). As for toxic shame, it's still pooling and swirling. On some occasions, mostly during weak moments, it gets the best of him. Old habits and negative ways of thinking seem to take over . . . and before he realizes it, he has lost the day spiritually.

Here's what's changed during his decade of walking with Jesus: He now doesn't try to hide his mess. He's pretty open about it, even writes songs about the stuff that trips him up. This brings sighs of relief in some who have heard his story: *I'm not alone!* they think. *I can stop pretending I have it all together and start living with authenticity, just like this guy. I don't have to be afraid anymore. I can take a step toward God, warts and all.*

Others, though, write off his life as yet another "depressing Seattle story" and even label him *hypocritical, phony, backslidden.*

I (Mike) am with the first group.

Even though my hang-ups differ, the fact is, I get hung up from time to time. Also a Christ-follower, I also don't have it all together.

I have a messy faith and a messy life.

I fall flat on my face—more often than I care to admit.

I desperately need a Savior.

The truth is we're all like "this guy," who once said:

This world is filled with wounded, hurting, broken souls. I'd say that we're *all* pretty messed up, but only a few are brave enough to admit it. We like to believe we're okay—that we have it all together. I've learned that it's okay to be broken. When we get to this point, we can put away all the junk that gets in the way—our efforts to "get things right," and do "Christian things." *God* is our Healer. He can accomplish in us what we cannot do on our own.

Wise words—and he has a lot more to say. Come meet Shane.

He's thirty-five now, and he encapsulates the essence of this book: He's a spiritual-loser-turned-winner who's relinquished formulas and "happy masks." He's learning how to get unstuck and to start living as God intends.

I recently sat down with Shane in an out-of-the-way coffeehouse. We sipped high-octane concoctions, had a few laughs, shared a few tears. We talked about life, faith, sin, forgiveness, and also the "dark sides" we all manage. He spoke of his path and what's helping him get unstuck these days.

He went all the way back to the beginning of the mess, telling a candid story about a rare yet most-vivid memory of his parents.

Four-year-old Shane pokes his head out from a fuzzy Scooby-Doo blanket and squints in the darkness. Something had wakened him—an eerie laugh . . . or maybe it was a moan. Ghosts? I bet *this* house is *haunted*.

He sniffs the air. Something doesn't smell right either. It's a mixture of dead flowers and Grandpa's pipe. Definitely ghosts.

"Mom?" he calls in the dark. "Are you awake? I'm really scared and—" He stops midsentence. Another noise downstairs.

Shane runs his hand over the spot his black lab usually fills but only makes contact with a Hot Wheel and a candy wrapper. "Sammy!" he calls. "Sammy, come here!" The hyper pup usually greets him now with a spongy tongue and a face full of slimy kisses. Instead—silence.

Shane climbs out and tiptoes to his parents' room. He peeks in, notices it's empty. Am I home alone?

He tiptoes to the winding staircase. His eyes grow big as he examines the shadows cast along the stairwell. The floor is fitted with gray stones; stained-glass windows with scary ancient faces line the outside wall. The family's century-old farmhouse feels like a creepy vampire's lair—especially at night.

He slides his hand along a rough wooden railing, takes a couple of steps. Suddenly . . . squeeeek! His foot on a chew toy, the boy gasps, frozen in his tracks, his heart playing keyboard with his rib cage. *Stupid dog*, he muses. *Where are you?*

Another step . . . a fourth, a fifth . . . eventually he reaches the bottom. Perfectly still, barely breathing—just like ninjas in his cartoons—Shane hugs a wall and listens. He hears voices from the living room. Undistinguishable words and laughing. The clink of a glass. The air is smoky and putrid.

He coughs and rubs his nose. Then he rolls his head around the corner and peeks in with one eye.

Just a few feet away, his parents lounge on a green shag rug by a coffee table. His dad is swaying and laughing—his shirt off, his frizzy brown hair pulled into a ponytail. He's taking turns with other half-naked people breathing smoke from a tube that connects to a glass contraption.

Shane turns away. A smoke-filled room . . . dirty-looking, tattooed strangers . . . his parents with them—laughing? They never laugh. They only yell and curse at each other—and at him.

Shane spins around and peeks into the room again. This time he catches his father's eye. The mirth is completely gone; the face is enraged. Shane knows what will happen next.

Yelling. Cursing.

The stinging slap of a rough hand.

The painful words: "I don't want you here."

The Mysteries Inside

A few days later Shane's parents dumped him off at his grandmother's with personal things stuffed into a trash bag: a mishmash of clothes, toys, crayons, coloring books, and the prized Scooby-Doo blanket.

"I guess Mom and Dad were following the times," he said. He sipped his coffee and leaned back in his chair. "They were self-absorbed hippies who lived for drugs and parties. But whatever their hang-ups, it was cruel to throw out a child with the garbage. *Unthinkable!* That's what they did to me."

I nodded. "That's one word; a few other choice phrases come to mind."

Shane cracked a smile. "Believe me—I've used *those* words too."

"Your story is painful. And amazing," I said. "I can't help but wonder, though: How does a boy—let alone a man—deal with this kind of rejection?"

"I was a confused kid who grew into a confused man," he said. "I was very insecure because I always felt different. *There's got to be something wrong with me,* I'd often think. *Am I unlovable? Is there something that makes others not want me?* I still battle with those questions today. But anger and hate ruled my life as a kid. I grew into a punk who hated authority and anyone over age twenty. I was cocky, rebellious, and extremely reckless."

"Which is why you followed in your parents' footsteps."

Shane looked me in the eye and swallowed. "Ironic, isn't it?" He looked down and paused for a moment, his fingers fiddling with a spoon. "I turned out just like the ones I hated so much. You name the drug, I was selling it and doing it—it's a long, ugly list. I even ended up getting a divorce—something I was determined never to let happen to me."

"But some obvious things have changed for you," I pointed out. "You really aren't your parents. What helped you turn things around?"

He looked up again. "Realizing that God forgives me and loves me exactly the way I am. I don't have to perform or try to be someone different. He wants me to be *me*. I got to that realization when I was at the lowest point ever, a deep hole. I was arrested and facing heavy charges. Behind bars, I began to accept the obvious: Something was desperately wrong with me. I started questioning my whole existence: *Who am I? Why am I here? What am I going to do with my life?* There were so many unanswered mysteries inside.

"After I was released from jail, a Christian friend began inviting me to church. He told me about the peace he'd found. I acted as though I was listening but really wasn't. I thought his story sounded really boring. Yet I was enticed by spirituality and, at the time, I was dabbling with the Rastafarian movement and Hinduism. Bob Marley was a huge idol of mine."

"Thankfully, your friend wasn't judgmental—and *was* persistent. Right?"

"Actually, I made life pretty hard for him. He'd constantly point me to Scripture and would invite me to church, and I'd constantly give him a lot of attitude. Two weeks before I committed my life to the Lord, he confessed his frustration with God. He told me how he'd prayed, 'I don't get it, Lord. I've poured my life into this kid. I don't understand why you don't lead him to you.' But something finally clicked inside, and *I* ended up praying something like this: 'God, I don't know who you are or where you are, but I need to find you. Whoever you are, show yourself to me. Give me a sign.'"

"Did God answer that prayer?"

"Yes—in a BIG way," Shane said. "Flipping through an old Bible, I began reading a passage from Matthew. I sensed the Lord telling me to clean the drugs out of my life, so I immediately got rid of everything. One day later, the police arrived with a search warrant. I was clean and didn't get arrested. I was convinced then that God really cares about me."

I smiled. "And everything turned out 'happily ever after'!"

Shane laughed. "Actually, that's when I began the really hard part—becoming a Christ-follower and letting God clean up my spiritual life. It's something He's still doing . . . will continue doing the rest of my life."

"I heard that after you committed your life to Him, your thirst for God seemed as out of control as your past drug use," I said. "Is that true?"

"Exactly right. I was consumed with studying the Bible. In the midst of all this, I started writing worship songs, and my friends encouraged me to perform them. I had this beat-up guitar I'd play at church. I'd perform worship songs every Sunday, and eventually, I started getting invitations all around the Pacific Northwest. So I started doing the coffeehouse thing, and little by little, my music seemed to catch on. But I think it's my story that surprises a lot of people: I'm a Christ-follower, yet I don't have it all together. What I do have is God's forgiveness for my sins and the promise of eternal life with Him."

Again, Shane still plays that beat-up guitar. The more his "yard-sale reject" delivers beautiful music, the more he feels a connection with it.

Yes, his life is still messy.

Yes, he still gets spiritually stuck from time to time.

But—through Christ—he's learning to grow.

"My faith is a learning process," he said. "My music is a way of talking with God. It's prayer. So my hope as a Christ-follower is to journey with people and to grow with them as I grow too."

Welcome to the Human Race

Turn to the book of Judges for snapshot after snapshot of uncensored *messes*—the dark side of humankind—along with God's gracious deliverance: "Then the Israelites did evil in the eyes of the Lord and served the Baals."[2] Keep reading and you will see that, despite gross human unfaithfulness, *God is faithful*. He molds and disciplines His children through persistent, unwearied love and matchless, absolutely underserved grace: "Then the Lord raised up judges, who saved them out of the hands of these raiders."[3]

In His perfect time, He will give a new beginning to those who'd once turned their backs to Him. The Bible says, "All have sinned and fall short of the glory of God."[4] It also *doesn't* say, "All who come to faith won't struggle anymore with sin and won't continue to need a Savior."[5]

Our sin nature and our specific sins are minute-by-minute reminders that our whole race has the same disease. Getting unstuck spiritually includes accepting this fact. While we don't want to sin so as to abuse grace, we're still in these temporary bodies and we're still bound to face temptation, so there's a sense in which we're still stuck with the muck. In this life that will never fully change, no matter how much we wish it would. We do want to learn how to resist temptation and overcome sin, but there's no success to be found in attempting to hide our condition from others (or ourselves).

What marks those who trust Jesus as Savior and Lord isn't the ability or certainty to sin less but the awareness of sin being forgiven and of being released from its ongoing consequences (guilt and shame). The experience of that freedom fills our hearts with love for God, for what He has done on our undeserving behalf; this love empowers us to serve Him by loving others.

Learning how to forget what lies behind[6] frees us to throw off the sin that so easily entangles us.[7] Getting unstuck means humbly asking God—regularly—to clean out the pipeline between Him and me and then starting again fresh. What does He say about yesterday's failure? "I will forgive their wickedness and will remember their sins no more."[8]

It's been said that half the people in psychiatric wards could go home if they knew they were forgiven. That's the power of knowing you're clean; the alternative is living with shame that affects your ability to live well today.

We're not content or at peace while mired in soul-harming behaviors. The primary focus of morality is for us to quit thinking about how to gratify ourselves (which usually leads to sin) and instead pondering how to serve others. Sinning less isn't a badge of honor—the credit goes to God. It's *His* amazingly powerful grace that enables us to move away from self-obsession and forward into love. Those who don't yet know Jesus won't be drawn to Him by our selfish and prideful attempts to highlight the "accomplishments" of our own efforts (which the apostle Paul called "rubbish"[9]). People can't relate to moral perfection—real or imagined—any more than we could have any connection to a perfect God without what *He* has done.

Accepting that we have a sin nature is hugely beneficial to keeping us humble and close to Christ. I like Charles Spurgeon's take on the heart's desperate state and God's healing touch:

What a mass of hideous sickness Jesus must have seen. Yet He was not disgusted but patiently healed them all. What a variety of evils He must have seen. What sickening ulcers and festering sores. Yet He was prepared for every type of evil and was victorious over its every form. . . . In every corner of the field, He triumphed over evil and received honor from the delivered captives. He came, He saw, He conquered everywhere. . . . Whatever my case may be, the beloved Physician can heal me. Whatever the state of others whom I remember in prayer, I have hope in Jesus that they will be healed. My child, my friend or my dearest one, I have hope for each and all when I remember the healing power of my Lord. In my own situation, however severe my struggle with sin and infirmities, I too may be of good cheer. He who on earth walked the hospitals still dispenses His grace and works wonders among His children. Let me earnestly go to Him at once.[10]

Now It's Your Turn: Engage, Untangle . . . *Grow!*

Read John 5:39–40. The Jewish priests—men who'd committed their lives to studying Scripture and to seeking God's Son—met the Messiah face-to-face yet rejected Him. They distrusted Jesus because He didn't fit their human definition of how the Ultimate Role Model should look and behave.

Read the following and jot down your impressions of Jesus.

- John 15:13–17_____
- Matthew 9:35–36_____
- Colossians 1:13–20_____
- Revelation 3:20–22_____
- John 1:32–36_____

If Jesus truly is everything you've described, isn't it time to start trusting Him, seeking Him, and thereby getting your faith growing again?
Write a prayer to Jesus, expressing that desire:

_____

_____

Write your definition of TRUE CHRISTIANITY:

_____

_____

Reread Philippians 2:8; then read Romans 6:9–11.

- In what way do we also "die"?
- What responsibility do we have in our "deaths"? (Read Romans 6:11–14 for a giant hint.)

As you seek healing and wholeness, wait patiently for the Lord.

God is never in a hurry. Then when He speaks to you—as He will—do what He tells you. It generally comes through your own conscience—a sort of growing conviction that such and such a course of action is the one He wants you to take. Or it may be given you in the advice of friends of sound judgment—those you love the most. God speaks sometimes through our circumstances and guides us, closing doors as well as opening them. He will let you know what you must do, and what you must be. He is waiting for you to touch Him (see Mark 5:31). The hand of faith is enough. Your trembling fingers can reach Him as He passes. Reach out your faith—touch Him. He will not ask, "Who touched me?" He will know.[11]

———◈———

Research Reveals: We're most likely to become effectively un-stuck—to experience lasting change—through an intentional, ongoing growth *process* based in *personal connection* with God. (To begin, we recommend engaging Him at least four days a week for a minimum of forty consecutive days).

Encouraging Nudge: *"All* are broken, but only a few admit it." The truth is, God doesn't expect us to have it all together. *He is our Healer;* according to His plan, our restoration will be complete in the end at the time of His choosing. There is nothing He desires in us that He can't accomplish in us. He'll clean out what weighs us down, including our tendency to do "what we do not want to do."[12]

Take a look at unstuck.gotandem.com for more practical ways to grow spiritually. Do this every day during your forty-five-day journey.

Spiritual
Stepping Stones

● DAy 34

Scripture to Remember: Romans 7:7–25

Question to Consider: With Christ's help, what struggle must I confront?

● DAy 35

Scripture to Remember: 1 Corinthians 10:1–13

Question to Consider: God promises a way of escape from temptation so that I can endure it. What new steps will I begin taking in order to enable success against the struggles I've faced repeatedly?

● DAy 36

Scripture to Remember: Hebrews 2:11–18

Question to Consider: Jesus, who also was tempted, understands what I'm going through. Does this truth help me to look Him in the eye when I sin? (Why, or why not?)

● **DAY 37**

Scripture to Remember: 1 John 1:1–10

Question to Consider: Despite my messes, Jesus, who died for my sins and has given me eternal life, won't reject me. Does this or will this change (1) how I feel about myself and (2) how I relate to others?

thirteen

Getting Unstuck Again . . . and *Again*

If someone has a hundred sheep and one of them wanders off, doesn't he leave the ninety-nine and go after the one? And if he finds it, doesn't he make far more over it than over the ninety-nine who stay put? Your Father in heaven feels the same way. He doesn't want to lose even one of these simple believers.[1]

—Jesus Christ

Filled with the Holy Spirit, Jesus journeys deep into the wilderness for intense "spiritual training." The Savior spends forty days and nights trekking through Judean wastelands alone, with no food or shelter. It's savage, desolate terrain, a dangerous place. The nights are bone-chillingly cold. By midday the sun's heat grows intolerable.

Weary and fighting the dull ache of starvation, Jesus begins the Test.

He's resting in a shady spot, the shadow of a boulder. His eyes are closed as He leans against the giant stone. Suddenly He senses an icy presence, the imminence of evil.

The Lord raises His head and squints. A few feet away, a flash of white light rises toward the sky, a radiance of super-natural power. Slowly coming into focus in the light's center is the image of a handsome man.

In a tone both arrogant and almost sympathetic, it speaks: "Since you are God's Son, speak the word that will turn these stones into loaves of bread."[2]

Jesus, neither standing nor yet answering, regards the light as a vicious beast. He closes His eyes again and whispers hoarsely: "It is written, 'Man shall not live on bread alone, but on every word that comes from the mouth of God.'"[3]

At once the iciness engulfs Him. A wind arises and howls. The Lord opens His eyes, sees the immersive light canceling the desert in a pale fog, and feels a footing beneath. He stands and the light releases Him, moving to one side; He has been transported to the highest corner of the temple wall.

Scattered below is Jerusalem. The priests blow trumpets to usher in the coming year. The air is thin; the height can induce faintness of heart.[4]

The icy light speaks again, resumes its prodding directive: "Since you are God's Son, jump."[5] The presence goads Him, quoting Psalm 91: "For the Scriptures declare, 'God will send His angels to keep You from harm'—they will prevent You from smashing on the rocks below."[6]

Jesus counters with truth from Deuteronomy: "It also says not to put the Lord your God to a foolish test!"[7]

In a flash the Holy City vanishes; Jesus, no longer on the wall, now is on a cosmic mountain, infinitely higher than anything made by human hands. The presence gestures ex-pansively, showcasing earth's kingdoms and proclaiming their glory. Then he says, "They're yours—lock, stock, and barrel. Just go down on your knees and worship me, and they're yours."[8]

But Jesus does not look, and His refusal is stern: "I know you. I know exactly what you are. Satan, tempter, betrayer— get away from Me."[9] The Creator of those kingdoms and all else backs His rebuke with more truth from the same Source: "Worship the Lord your God, and only Him. Serve Him with absolute single-heartedness."[10]

Instantly Jesus is in the desert again, leaning against a boulder. The Test is over; the devil is gone. In place of the icy presence are warmth and peace and goodness. Angels from heaven are here to care for the Savior.[11]

Putting on Your Protective Armor

Imagine the stress. If Jesus had slipped up, had committed even a "little sin," it would have been over. There wouldn't have been a Perfect Sacrifice to live and die in our place—and the world would not have been saved. Satan, knowing this, used all his strength and cunning to get Jesus to stumble.

Jesus had been in the wilderness nearly six weeks with no food. Naturally, He was struggling. The devil's first phase of attack was the temptation of immediate self-gratification.

"If you are the Son of God, tell these stones to become bread." (Let your physical desires take control. You deserve what you want: your way, right away.)

When the ruse failed, Satan tried phase two: If you're legit, step off the edge—God says the angels will provide a safe landing. (Prove your power. Show me you're a tough guy; take a risk. Or . . . are even you full of doubts?)

And then phase three, for the big prize: From a high mountain, Satan showed him all the kingdoms of the world. "All

this I will give you, if you will bow down and worship me."
(You can have it all if you only reorder your allegiance. Just
a tiny compromise and you'll have it made. A small white lie
hardly counts, and it'd take all the pressure off. Cheat just a
little so you can pass.)

Satan attacked hard and heavy. But even though Jesus was
thoroughly exhausted, He won. How? The Word of God is
powerful ammunition.

There's definite supernatural power in Scripture. Ephesians
lists the "armor" we're to wear when stepping into battle
against the enemy—in light of how challenging life is, that
can pretty much start the moment we wake in the morning.
While most items are defensive, we're given the one offensive
weapon we need: "the sword of the Spirit, which is the word
of God."[12]

Paul's powerful metaphor of a Christ-follower's armor
wraps truth into something easily remembered when enticements strike.[13] But it's the truth behind the metaphor that
brings us the victory. Putting on God's armor means working
the metaphor's truth into our lives through consistent Bible
engagement—in this case, especially meditative thought.

True Jesus-following is about living truth in the now.

It's about enjoying Jesus every moment and facing each attack as it comes to ward off *anything* that threatens a breach.
And if we don't appreciate the moment-by-moment nature of
relationship with Him, we tend to spend a lot of time blaming
God for not answering our prayers to take away sinful desires.

Learning to withstand in every battle as it dawns (that's
true spiritual maturity, by the way) isn't optional, at any rate,
because as long as we live on this earth, temptations will
keep coming.

Take up the shield of faith.

Jesus is our shield[14] and the Source of our faith.[15] Starting to get the picture? A believer's armor is nothing more or less than a multifaceted presentation of what Jesus does for us. *If we need protection from sin, then we need more of Jesus.* That's the upside of managing our "dark sides"—it pushes us to where we're desperate to experience more of Christ. When those burning darts start flying—an opportunity to overeat, a jolt of envy, the urge to gossip—we can raise our shields with a simple prayer: "Jesus, I need you!" Keep up the shield and keep fleeing temptation until those smoldering arrows are extinguished.

Take up the sword of the Spirit.

God's Word, our blade of truth,[16] can parry the devil's thrusts and stab his lies. The Spirit's sword has a keen edge leading to a deadly point. Wielded well, it can counterattack the enemy and slay temptation before it grows into an overpowering monster.

Put on the belt of truth.

A centurion's belt bonded his armor; he'd never consider fighting without it, because if he took that off, everything fell apart. It had to be tight, "girded up," ready for combat. *You need truth.* The better your grasp of Scripture, the stronger your belt buckle. Lacking truth, you're naked, easy pickings. Don't clutch and grab anyone or anything but Jesus—and hold tightly to Him, the living Truth,[17] to be ready.

Put on the breastplate of righteousness.

The breastplate covered the chest. Without it, a soldier was open to a thrust in the heart, which Satan targets. He tries to establish that you're wicked at the core and that you've no choice to be anything else. *Not true.* Because of Jesus Christ, God sees you as righteous![18] When you believe what God says—"I am righteous because of Jesus"—over Satan's accusations, over what anyone else says, and over your own contrary thoughts, your breastplate is firmly in place to protect you from stabs at your very identity.

Put on the gospel of peace (your combat boots).

A centurion's boots were broken in and carefully treated, as much a comfort during long days of travel as a protection in conflict. Many people think the Christian walk is exhausting and impossible (especially in terms of temptation and sin). But the message of Jesus is the good news of *peace*:

> Come to me, all you who are weary and burdened, and I will give you rest. Take my yoke upon you and learn from me, for I am gentle and humble in heart, and you will find rest for your souls. For my yoke is easy and my burden is light.[19]

Rest? Easy? Light?

If we're convinced the essence of the Christian life is *wearisome, arduous, heavy,* that's exactly what we'll experience. In those moments of navel-gazing discouragement, we're without our combat boots, barefoot over thorny and rocky ground. Connect with Jesus—He's everything we need. *Our truth. Our righteousness. Our peace. Our rest.* The path into spiritual maturity isn't short, and sometimes it's uphill, but it's an adventure we're to enjoy.

Put on the helmet of salvation.

Do we think Jesus came only to save us from hell? There's so much more to it. For one thing, He came to save us from *ourselves.* His death handled the eternity part; His life is an ongoing miracle of salvation from the sinful cravings with which we were born.[20] Salvation is abundant life, His gift to us,[21] and *life doesn't begin after we leave earth for what's beyond!* Every minute we're enjoying abundance, our helmet is on, and with it firmly in place our minds are guarded from Satan's veil.[22]

Embrace Healing: No More Arms Around Sin

Whether we're entangled in a soul-robbing addiction or suffer from a lying tongue, all sin grows the same way:

> When tempted, no one should say, "God is tempting me." For God cannot be tempted by evil, nor does he tempt anyone; but each person is tempted when they are dragged away by their own evil desire and enticed. Then, after desire has conceived, it gives birth to sin; and sin, when it is full-grown, gives birth to death.[23]

Wisdom is allowing God to uproot the problem and bring any darkness into the light, accepting His forgiveness, and letting Him do His healing work—which is sometimes painful and often humbling. Sadly, these aren't the steps we usually take. Despite the reality of sin in every believer's life—and despite its deadly consequences—far too many of us drive sin underground and refuse to deal with it.

That's basically insane, when you think about it.

We can be free from the bondage of sin, *and* we have the promise of eternal life with our heavenly Father, who's absolutely crazy in love with us. All we must do is stop pretending we have it all together, admit the stuff that's gotten us stuck, step into repentance, and then trust that God will do His part.

When we fake it, David Wilkerson says, we bring others down with us:

We stigmatize people with life-controlling problems. We take away their character by thinking of them as hopelessly hooked. We are so offended by their practices, we have made their sins so scandalous, we turn them into outcasts with no hope of return. We help to destroy their hunger for God by bringing down on them an avalanche of reproach and unforgiving wrath.

If you rob a sinner of his character, if you take away his dignity, if you focus only on his failures, if you treat him as a nonperson, if you shut off all his roads of retreat—he is driven to hardness. He becomes calloused and begins to fight back because that is all that is left for him. It is an easy step from hardness to violence. Humiliate the sinner, take away his sense of worth, and soon you will have driven him to [unrepentant] total remorse. If there is no God in him to support him, he will lose all hope and finally give himself over to those who accept him. Then he often uses that hostility as an excuse to remain in his sin.[24]

The Bible, from its first page to the last, challenges believers to overcome sin—counting themselves dead to sin and alive in Christ.

Do not let sin reign in your mortal body so that you obey its evil desires. Do not offer any part of yourself to sin as an instrument of wickedness, but rather offer yourselves to God as those who have been brought from death to life; and offer every part of yourself to him as an instrument of righteousness. For sin shall no longer be your master, because you are not under the law, but under grace.[25]

Now It's Your Turn: Engage, Untangle . . . *Grow!*

Deceit always accompanies temptation and sin.

In other words, we convince ourselves we're doing nothing wrong when, in fact, we are. According to addiction recovery expert Patrick Means, "When we want something badly enough, we'll deceive whomever we have to in order to get it. And the first person we have to deceive is ourselves." He says we accomplish self-deceit by telling ourselves two lies: (1) "I don't really have a problem," and (2) "I can handle this alone."[26]

List three examples of when you've told yourself these lies. Then, across from each lie, list a way you could have broken the self-deception cycle.

Lie: _____ Truth Step: _____

Lie: _____ Truth Step: _____

Lie: _____ Truth Step: _____

Some of us have problems visible to everyone around us. Some of us have problems but work doggedly to keep them all secret. Some of us have visible *and* secret problems. No matter the "category," no one is problem-free, and while we could discuss the reasons we try not to look problem-ridden (or try to look perfect) till the end of time, the main point in doing so is both disingenuous and ruinous. Living out this lie carries terrible costs for the Christ-follower—broken trust, diminishing intimacy, wrecked credibility, vulnerability to accusations of hypocrisy, and worst of all, insensitivity to God's Spirit and inability to connect with Him.

If you're keeping sin secret, don't let yourself go a day pretending it won't come back to bite you. If you don't start allowing the power of God's grace to control sin now, why would you think you can control sin's consequences when they show up?

Create a plan for giving up sins.

Confess. This is the healing answer to crippled faith, the way to bring your struggles into God's light. You don't have to live with a huge load of guilt and shame. Christ is reaching out to you with open arms. Go to Him prayerfully; tell Him all about the secrets He already knows. "If we confess our sins, he is faithful and just and will forgive us our sins and purify us from all unrighteousness."[27]

Repent. Once you've confessed the sin(s) and asked Jesus to help you change (this is repentance), stop flogging yourself. You are totally forgiven. Now, your relationship with God restored, take steps toward change and growth. (The Holy Spirit will help you.)

Be warned: Avoid false repentance. Don't "confess" sin just to feel you've cleared a slate and can return to the sin you're planning tomorrow.

> When it comes to giving up a secret life, I believe there is a simple test to help us know whether we're experiencing true or false repentance. If I'm willing to tell someone else what I'm struggling with and ask for help, then it's true repentance. If I'm not willing to tell anyone else, I'm only fooling myself.[28]

Understand the battle being waged in your mind.

I'm hopeless—too far gone. I am what I am and will always be; I can't change. If you ever catch yourself thinking this, don't buy the lie whispered into your heart. When you do, again and again, you get trapped in a toxic shame cycle: You desperately want to change yet feel so innately flawed as to conclude that even if what God says is true about everyone else, *you* are beyond rescue. If you accept this, you're inviting Satan to hold you in bondage and keep you tripping over the same things every time you take a step.

There's a big difference between *guilt* and *shame*. Guilt has to do with our behavior, or what we do; shame has to do with our identity, or who we are.

When we do something wrong, our God-given conscience rings an alarm. That pang we feel is guilt. Guilt is not destructive to our person because we can do something about it. We can acknowledge our wrongdoing, change our behavior, experience forgiveness, and we no longer have to feel guilty. . . .

[Shame] pools and swirls outside the fringes of our lives like a poisonous nerve gas, waiting for us to open the door a crack and let it seep in to paralyze and destroy. Shame, in this sense, is a de-motivator for ongoing growth. It usually results in self-condemnation, discouragement, and the urge to give up.[29]

Shame rots and erodes. *I'm worthless. Yeah, no one's perfect, but I'm irredeemable. God will never accept me—even He can't help me.*

Shame causes us to expect the worst from ourselves because we believe that's intrinsically who we are, says Robert McGee: "We're not surprised when we disappoint people because deep down inside we know we're no good."[30] That's what makes shame toxic. Are you drinking poison?

If so, list three steps you will take to break free from toxic shame:

1.
2.
3.

Fight the enemy's lies.

Believe that Jesus Christ loves you and accepts you, no matter what your sin. Max Lucado simplifies "trusting God":

Take Jesus at His word. Learn that when He says something, it happens. When He says we're forgiven, let's unload the guilt [and, thereby, shame]. When He says we're valuable, let's believe Him. When He says we're provided for, let's stop worrying.[31]

List three ways in which you'll begin taking Jesus at His word:

1.
2.
3.

In the next chapter we'll consider ways to steer clear of formula faith and subculture Christianity.

Research Reveals: Sin doesn't happen in a vacuum. One person's sin affects others. It's the same with spiritual growth—one person's victory affects others too.

Encouraging Nudge: When we confess our sins, God forgets them completely: He erases the board, shreds the evidence, and hits Delete. Getting clean from the past is a wondrous way to start the day. And time with God *will* make a difference—remember: Taking our eyes off ourselves means we can love others more and better.

Take a look at unstuck.gotandem.com for more practical ways to grow spiritually. Do this every day during your forty-five-day journey.

Spiritual
Stepping Stones

● DAY 38

Scripture to Remember: Psalm 103:8–13

Question to Consider: Do I trust the Lord's compassion for me? Do I believe my sins are forgiven *and* forgotten?

● DAY 39

Scripture to Remember: Luke 7:36–50

Question to Consider: Have I been set free by Christ's love? Am I still holding on to past wounds?

● DAY 40

Scripture to Remember: Romans 3:9–20

Question to Consider: God says that because of Christ's sacrifice, He won't hold my sins against me. Admitting them and committing my life to Christ means I'll be spending it with Him, *forever.* Have I allowed this radical truth to transform my life here and now? (Take a few days to ponder this.)

● DAY 41

Scripture to Remember: Romans 5:12–21

Question to Consider: Through Christ I've found, and will keep finding, real life, real answers, real faith. Am I ready to stop stressing and start celebrating?

fourteen

Throwing Out the Formulas

Don't look for shortcuts to God. The market is flooded with surefire, easygoing formulas for a successful life that can be practiced in your spare time. Don't fall for that stuff, even though crowds of people do. The way to life—to God!—is vigorous and requires total attention.[1]

—Jesus Christ

Spiritual Perfection in Twenty-Four Hours . . . or We'll Sell You Something Else.

We've all heard (and we keep hearing) the newest promises from the latest *New York Times* bestsellers. However, most of today's churchgoers are jaded by empty-calorie McFaith hype and flat-out fed up with fast-food faith.

I (Mike) also cringe when I think about the subculture we've formed. We have our own record labels, radio networks, TV stations, educational systems, and political hierarchy. We manufacture our own lines of jewelry with crosses, purity rings, and tattoos. We bumper-sticker our cars with "I'm not perfect, just forgiven" next to magnetic fish symbols.

There are "Christian only" housing communities. Christian business owners give discounts to those who say "I'm a Christian" or "I work at [fill-in-the-blank] church/ministry." We have our own buzzwords (*cell group, worldview, megachurch, parachurch, born again, on fire*). The church we attend determines our status. Some of us even dress alike.

True story: When members of a women's activist group wanted to see the inside of their radically conservative archenemy's headquarters—which happened to be a popular Christian ministry—they arranged for a tour and arrived incognito . . . wearing outdated flowered dresses and clunky black shoes with their hair pulled back into buns. Apparently they assumed all "right-wing Christian ladies" had a thing for obnoxious retro fashion! (We can only assume they had previous experience on which to base the assumption.)[2]

The Real Reason We're Here

Now, please don't misunderstand: I have nothing against Christian ministries and media outlets. (I'm part of them.) The problem comes when—wait for it—we get stuck.

Bob Briner once compared the Christian church and its media subculture to a ghetto that the rest of society either avoids altogether or races through en route to another part of town. Briner was a shining, exemplary Christ-follower who avoided formula faith and lived out what he believed well beyond the church's fringes. He was convinced that the 24/7 pursuit of communicating the gospel happens most effectively through "countless ordinary people in countless ordinary ways in the real world."

He was frustrated. He wasn't sure if believers really understood this.

It's almost as if we believe God is strong enough to take care of His own only as long as they stay within the safety of the Christian ghetto. And yet, the Bible gives us countless examples of people like Joseph, who not only served as an advisor to the "president" of his day but also used that position to influence the entire land. Can't we do that today?[3]

Living our lives in a holy huddle and plugging in to formula faith makes us feel safe, even comfortable. And it's a whole lot smoother than the vigorous path Christ calls us to take. Philip Yancey observes:

> We want God to be like us: tangible, material, perceptible (hence the long history of idolatry). We want God to speak in audible words that we can clearly understand (Ezra Stiles of Yale studied Hebrew in order to converse with God in His native language).[4]

Yet as Yancey points out, God seeks from us correspondence in a spiritual realm and seems more interested in other kinds of growth: justice, mercy, peace, grace, and love—spiritual qualities that can work themselves out in a material world. In short, God wants us to be more like Him.[5]

I frequently find myself following the Christian crowd. My faith often *does* seem based on the most-recent big-Christian-author book. Sometimes I can't explain to someone why I believe in Jesus Christ, the Living Word, without using Christianese!

Maybe it's time to readjust my thinking.

Maybe it's time to give up formula faith.

Let's review.

Getting unstuck spiritually is NOT about . . .

. . . performance-based theologies or works-righteousness—that is, trying to gain acceptance from God by living up to a set of rules.

. . . always *feeling* close to God.

. . . mastering Bible-in-a-year plans, obsessively attending church, bringing God into every conversation, and otherwise attempting to build up enough tokens for our salvation.

. . . checking off daily lists of "sins avoided" and "good deeds accomplished."

. . . obeying God in order to be showered with His blessings.

. . . becoming "a better person" by following rules and rituals.

Getting unstuck spiritually IS about . . .

. . . letting go of the illusion that we're in control of life, faith, even God—and humbly accepting His forgiveness.

. . . trusting Jesus even when we don't sense His working in our lives.

. . . accepting the truth that He saved us, not on the basis of what we've done, but because of His mercy.[6]

. . . believing there's nothing we can do to earn God's love and nothing we can do to lose it.

. . . understanding that we cannot trick God. He can't be manipulated by good behavior. We're able to follow Him *because* He has freed us, not because we've merited it.

. . . living in a continual, growing relationship with Jesus Christ.

We Are His Body

Just as a body, though one, has many parts, but all its many parts form one body, so it is with Christ.[7]

Countless sermons, songs, and devotionals have been based on this verse. I'm usually distracted by trying to figure out which part of the body I am. I quickly think of the things I've done lately and try placing them into categories. Sometimes I chuckle as I think of odd parts I might be: the middle toe, the eyelash, the belly button. But if I step back, out of me-focus, a bigger picture is viewable. It's not just about our actions and where we fit in; it describes how we're designed specifically and intentionally by our Creator. We're not a bunch of random creatures thrown into this world to bump around and fumble our way through life. Each and every one of us has been designed in God's image. We all have a purpose; we fit together by His great design.

"Even the very hairs of your head are all numbered," said Jesus. "So don't be afraid."[8] Throughout human history *and* the future there won't ever be another "me." I'm unique, you're unique; each person who's ever lived is purposefully unique! We have things in common, like a body. We all need to breathe, eat, sleep. We all hunger to know God and want to live with a purpose. But we do so in our own unique way— because that's how we've been created.

> I am the good shepherd; I know my sheep and my sheep know me—just as the Father knows me and I know the Father—and I lay down my life for the sheep.[9]

Consider these four commonalities:

1. He created us.
2. He has saved us.
3. He loves us.
4. He pursues us every day.

The first three can be summed up with a clear understanding about God and what He's done for us. The fourth is more interactive; *He's* still pursuing, but we get to join in, take part in His story, run to Him as He runs toward us, and open our minds and hearts while adjusting our steps to follow His on the path.

Not only does God offer us a way of forgiveness and redemption, He also has provided us with the support and the tools that will draw us closer to Him. The Holy Scriptures are integral, and there's a reason so many refer to them as *Living*. God knew what He was doing when He spoke this way. Knowing how unique and different we all are, He reaches back through His Word and gives us the guidance and direction we need in our time and situation.

Leviticus 19:18 is a popular verse often referred to as the Golden Rule: "Do not seek revenge or bear a grudge against anyone among your people, but love your neighbor as yourself. I am the Lord." If a hundred of us read this, we'll have at least a hundred unique twists on its meaning.

And that's not necessarily wrong! If you're having troubles with your actual next-door neighbor, you may turn your focus to loving him instead of getting even. If you've wronged someone and she's forgiven you, these words might humble you before God and "neighbor" out of thankfulness. If a friend is seeking advice, you might be able to pass along a situational application of this godly wisdom as you share. Meditating on it may prompt someone to search his heart and ask God to cleanse him of any hidden resentment.

What's the limit on the number of ways God can speak to people—even the same person—through the same words? *Wherever* you are today, *whatever* you're doing today, *anything* you're considering today, *whomever* you're relating with today—God's Living Word will speak directly to it if you are living in the *now*; His voice through His story doesn't take days off.

The Lord meets us where we are with what we need. He doesn't change, and neither does truth. Though the actual printed words of Scripture have been the same for thousands of years, He speaks into our present moments according to His will to guide us, His creations.

If it sounds like a formula to say we should engage God's Word—and no doubt that first step *is* that straight-forward—let me say this: Once you start connecting with God through His living message to you, Scripture becomes personal, vibrant, an active voice with the wisest, soundest, most germane guidance in the most relevant conversation you could have with anyone, anywhere. God's creativity is inexpressibly, limitlessly powerful. As you welcome your Creator into your life, His words *will* become a life-changing influence. This goes eons beyond any formula we humans could ever design.

I'm quick to acknowledge this is hard to believe without experiencing it. So dive in headfirst. Listen. Explore. Discover. *Grow.*

Here are some of the ways Christians connect with God:

I Savor Coffee and Conversation: "Sometimes it happens in my office, sometimes at my favorite coffee spot. But it happens nearly every day—usually at different times. I open my Bible, sip something caffeinated, and have a conversation with my Creator. It involves reading, reflecting, praying . . . and listening." (*Brian, 52, Tulsa*)

I Get Alone With God: "I pray continually throughout the day—while holding my baby, preparing lunches for the kids, sending my husband off to work. But when my little one takes a nap, I seize those moments to read Scripture and to reflect on God's Word." (*Kate, 33, Fairfax, VA*)

I Take a Long Run on the Beach: "Before going to bed, I read a passage from the Bible, then I highlight a verse or two. When I get up in the morning, I pull on my running shoes and jog. I spend that time meditating on and memorizing the Scripture I highlighted." (*Tricia, 27, Virginia Beach*)

I Write Songs in the Evening: "Right after I tuck my kids into bed, I pick up my Bible and my guitar and head to our basement. I read, strum, and pray. Somewhere in the process I write a song . . . and connect with my Lord and Savior." (*Mark, 42, Brentwood, TN*)

I Dance With Jesus: "I was introduced to ballet practically the moment I learned to walk. Today I use it to bring glory to God. For me, dancing is a sacred, spiritual pursuit. I pray and communicate with my Creator during those moments—whether I'm onstage or alone with God during practice." (*Rachel, 22, Colorado Springs*)

I Prepare a Sunday School Lesson: "I pray for each student, study Scripture, and spend a lot of time sitting still, listening to God." (*Bob, 62, Lincoln, NE*)

I Journal on My Laptop: "I write out prayers to God, lists of people to pray for, Scriptures I'm memorizing . . . and just a whole bunch of random thoughts about my faith and my life. It's how I have my daily devos. I love looking back on stuff I wrote a year ago. It's fun to see how I've grown spiritually." (*Andrew, 16, San Diego*)

I Paint My Prayers: "I can't think of a better way to worship God than through art. I work in oils, and the things I paint represent my prayers and hopes. After meditating on a passage from God's Word—sometimes just one verse—I dip my brush onto my pallet and begin to create. I talk to Jesus during those moments. At times I laugh and sing; at other moments, I cry. I usually come away from an art session feeling more connected to God." (*David, 48, Arcata, CA*)

I Reflect on the Word During Train Rides Into the City: "I read a passage or two, then I look out the window and pray. As the Manhattan skyscrapers come into view, my mind floods with people to talk to God about, along with my own fears and dreams. Those moments never fail to bring me closer to Jesus." (*Vanessa, 47, Rockville, NY*)

I Grow As I Work in the Garden: "I love my garden. In fact, I call my flower-filled Southwest ranch *Beulah*: a name symbolically applied to Israel.[10] As I plant things and trim hedges, I worship my Creator. I often meditate on God's Word and pray. It always becomes a beautiful two-way conversation." (*Amie, 72, Albuquerque*)

As these folks have demonstrated, winning the day spiritually is about a personal connection with Jesus that builds a foundation of *right thinking* and *genuine belief*. Faith begins with belief, and again, it deepens as we respond to Christ's invitation: "Love the Lord your God with all your heart and with all your soul and with all your mind and with all your strength."[11]

Now It's Your Turn: Engage, Untangle . . . *Grow!*

Gear up for the long haul.

Here's how Hebrews describes spiritual growth: "Let us throw off everything that hinders . . . and let us run with perseverance the race marked out for us."[12] Even if we've survived spiritual immaturity until now, eventually we all have to grow up. Getting unstuck and learning to grow up is like an ultramarathon that continues for the rest of our lives.

Plot a growth course. List some goals. Suggestions:

In one month I want to:

In six months I want to:

In one year I want to:

Don't forget: Spiritual growth is a choice.

You had no choice to be born. Childhood came without your consideration. Becoming a Christ-follower and growing in faith is different. You have to choose faith, and to choose you must exercise your will. If you don't choose spiritual growth, you'll remain a toddler believer.

Paul, a bright example of a mature Christ-follower because he bravely chose to act like one, said: "Be on your guard; stand firm in the faith; be courageous; be strong."[13] That's a command that requires a choice, a firm act of volition to obey; no lazy mind, weak will, or halfheartedness allowed.

When you walk this way, on this path, you will not be disappointed. Do you know what comes after brokenness? Healing. You can count on it!

Paul drew a clear contrast between kids and adults with these words: "When I was a child, I talked like a child, I thought like a child, I reasoned like a child. When I became a man, I put the ways of childhood behind me."[14]

Choices you will make to grow and to reach goals:

1.
2.
3.
4.
5.
6.
7.
8.
9.
10.

It's amazing how, during hard moments, a certain verse can pop into your head. The Lord will use it to strengthen you and to throw off Satan. Try memorizing Scripture that, for example, tells how God has conquered fear:

> This is love for God: to keep his commands. And his commands are not burdensome, for everyone born of God overcomes the world. This is the victory that has overcome the world, even our faith. Who is it that overcomes the world? Only the one who believes that Jesus is the Son of God.[15]

Verses/passages you plan to memorize during the next year:

1.
2.
3.
4.
5.
6.

7.

8.

9.

10.

11.

12.

———◉———

Twenty-six-year-old Jill from Nashville says:

I've asked God to break me. It seems like an odd request, and it's been a painful one. And yet, I'm finding that God has been meeting me every place I've been. My faith has been built up so much. Through it all, do you know what I've discovered? We need other Christians. It's okay to lean on someone when we feel weak. To truly become who God wants us to be, we need a body of believers.

Consider starting an accountability group or an accountability relationship with just one person. List people you'd like to talk with about this. Consider: How often will you meet? What will be your expectations?

———◉———

Research Reveals: Mature believers say relationship with Jesus means personal, two-way communication, which involves trust, commitment, and authenticity. Intimacy and growth are inseparable.

Encouraging Nudge: Put away preconceived notions about what it means to get unstuck spiritually. The Lord wants a personal friendship—an intimate, eternal relationship—with each of us. He searches out all our thoughts and knows our words before they're spoken. He's *never* unavailable to walk with us and talk with us!

Take a look at unstuck.gotandem.com for more practical ways to grow spiritually. Do this every day during your forty-five-day journey.

Spiritual
Stepping Stones

● DAY 42

Scripture to Remember: 1 Chronicles 29:10–20

Question to Consider: Based upon the message of these verses, what should I view as my real home . . . *my true treasure?*

● DAY 43

Scripture to Remember: Psalm 139

Question to Consider: I am not an accident. I'm a unique creation God placed here for a purpose of His design. Do I truly believe this—even when I feel stuck? How does this truth help me to get unstuck?

● DAY 44

Scripture to Remember: Psalm 145

Question to Consider: How can I remain fearful or overwhelmed by life's pressures when the Lord is very near? (How can I be lifted up by Him?)

● DAY 45

Scripture to Remember: Isaiah 26

Question to Consider: Serving God now on earth and then forever in heaven involves key steps every believer must take. We're to know God intimately, loving Him and loving our neighbors! Read Isaiah 26 (written as a song of praise for God's deliverance). What do I feel when I read verses 1–15? What are some ways in which I can live these verses?

Appendix 1

Four Critical Elements of Spiritual Growth

The Knowledge Element

- *Receive God's Word:* Hearing from God through the Bible is foundational to becoming spiritually mature. (Luke 4:16; John 5:39; Acts 15:30–31; Colossians 4:16)
- *Reflect on God's Word:* Meditation and reflection on what we've read pave the way for understanding. (Joshua 1:8; Psalm 1:1–2; 119:15–16; 1 Timothy 4:15)
- *Understand God's Word:* Reading without understanding is futile. (Nehemiah 8:2–3, 8, 13; Psalm 119:27; Proverbs 2:1–6)

The Prayer Element

- *Prepare our hearts:* We do this through reflection and confession. (Deuteronomy 6:5; Psalm 10:17; 34:18; 51:10)

- *Manage our environment:* The disciplines of solitude, silence, and stillness enhance our intimacy with God through prayer. (Psalm 46:10; Zechariah 2:13; Matthew 14:23; Luke 6:12)
- *Pray in the way of the Word:* An evidence of spiritual maturity is approaching God in the biblical way. (1 Kings 18:36–37; 2 Kings 19:14–19; Nehemiah 1:4–11; Matthew 6:9–13)

The Faith Element

- *Trust God's Word:* Trusting the Bible's credibility, integrity, and veracity is crucial to a desire to engage it and respond to it. (Psalm 18:30; 119:160; Proverbs 30:5; 2 Timothy 3:16)
- *Believe God's Word:* Faith in God and His Word must become a personal matter, or it's merely an academic exercise. (Deuteronomy 1:29–33; 2 Chronicles 20:20; Luke 8:11–12; John 5:38–39)
- *Internalize God's Word:* Making the Bible our own, metabolizing God's Word, enables Scripture to be the active ingredient in our spiritual growth. (Psalm 119:11; Ezekiel 3:1–3; Jeremiah 15:16; 1 Corinthians 13:11)

The Action Element

- *Live out God's Word:* The ultimate goal of engaging God's Word is obedience; obedience is evidence of spiritual growth. (Psalm 119:67, 71; Matthew 4:4; Philippians 2:12–13; 1 Timothy 4:12; James 1:22–24)

- *Share God's Word:* One discipline of spiritually mature people is evangelization. (Acts 4:1–4; 8:4, 25; 13:49; 17:22–23)
- *Flourish in God's Word:* Being fruitful (or effective) in our Christian life is an indication of spiritual maturity. (Psalm 1:1–3; 92:12–15; Proverbs 12:12; Matthew 7:17)

Appendix 2

Our Research Methods

By Dr. Pamela Ovwigho

If you look carefully, you'll notice research is everywhere these days. Good research can help us make better decisions and live better lives; bad research can lead to just the opposite. So it's important to consider the reliability and validity of findings from any particular study.

Reliable means the extent to which studies yield the same results on repeated trials. *Valid* means the extent to which a concept, conclusion, or measurement is well-founded and corresponds accurately to the real world.

How do we know if a study is reliable and valid? By examining how the research was done. Here are some questions to demonstrate more about our research and to guide you in examining any study you may encounter.

Who was included in the study?

A simple research rule: the more cases included in a study, the more reliable its findings. You can have more confidence in a study based on a thousand surveys than one based on fifty. Multiple studies with thousands of people all producing the same results demonstrate even more reliability and validity.

It's also important to consider participants' gender, age, ethnicity, religious preference, and so on. For example, how, and how often, a group of sixty-year-old, church-attending women engages the Bible is likely quite different from how, and how often, a group of thirty-year-old men do.

The findings presented in *Unstuck* are based on data from more than seventy thousand Americans who completed surveys between 2005 and 2011. Some surveys focused on specific groups; e.g., people who attend church regularly. Others draw from a random sample of the population. Regardless of which group we studied, in one regard the results were the same: Consistently engaging the Bible made a marked difference in people's spiritual lives.

How was the study conducted?

Generally, social science research can be quantitative or qualitative. (CBE does both.) *Qualitative* involves asking open-ended questions where the participant can answer in his or her own words. Responses are then analyzed for common themes. In our CBE research, for instance, we like to ask: "How does God communicate with you?" Answers typically show a wide variety.

> *"He provides me and my family with jobs and good health to buy food and pay bills, and have material things so we can live our lives comfortably."*
> *"He watches over me."*
> *"By keeping me healthy and safe."*
> *"Through a feeling."*

*"He gives me a good feeling in my heart and lets me know
He loves me."*

"Through thoughts in my head."

*"He shows me His will through Scripture and through
events in my life. He speaks to my heart/soul."*

In *quantitative* studies, researchers typically ask multiple-choice questions with numbers assigned to each response. For instance, we ask how many days people have read or listened to the Bible in the past week; they give a number between zero and seven. We may ask how often they attend church and give choices like "weekly," "a couple of times a month," "about once a month," "a few times a year," "only on special occasions," or "never."

Such data allows for greater flexibility in using statistical models to analyze the results. The tricky part, especially for attempts to measure factors like spiritual growth, is measuring the unseen. Surveys need to be constructed carefully; questions must be worded in ways that are clear, concise, and don't bias responses. Researchers also have developed means to include questions that detect if people may be answering in a biased way, like wanting to present an idealized self-image or wanting to please the researcher.

What other explanations were considered?

In a way, researchers are trained to think upside down—that is, we enter a study assuming that the phenomenon under examination makes absolutely no difference in a person's life. This is called the null hypothesis, which, in this case, for CBE, was "There is no difference in the behavior of people who engage the Bible most days of the week compared to those who do not engage the Bible." The burden of proof is to show that whatever the researcher is examining makes more of a difference than can be explained by chance alone.

Throughout this book we've made the following statement confidently:

Spiritually and behaviorally speaking, we found nothing that comes close to having the impact of the Bible on the spiritual lives of those who engage it.

A *very* bold declaration, especially coming from researchers taught to be cautious and use language that hedges, such as "it appears," "most likely," and "we hypothesize." But our confidence is founded in our having repeatedly tested Bible engagement's effect, with a wide variety of people, using multivariate statistical models that allow testing one factor while statistically controlling for other factors that may also explain differences in behavior.

Dr. Pamela Ovwigho, CBE's executive director, assisted Arnie Cole with the research presented in this book.

Notes

Dedication

1. C. S. Lewis, "Giving All to Christ," *Devotional Classics,* eds., Richard J. Foster and James Bryan Smith (New York: HarperCollins, 1990), 8.

Chapter 1: Confessions of a Spiritual Loser

1. www.ThinkExist.com, "William Arthur Ward Quotes" (© 1999–2010).
2. Psalm 63:1
3. Quoted in Tom Stephen and Virginia Starkey, *Fearless* (Ventura, CA: Regal, 2006), 2.
4. Brennan Manning, *Posers, Fakers, and Wannabes* (Colorado Springs: NavPress, 2003), 21.
5. 2 Timothy 3:16–17 *The Message*
6. Dr. Norman Geisler, from a lecture titled "The Bible: Uniqueness of Its Composition," delivered in Lincoln, Nebraska (05/01/09).
7. Eugene H. Peterson, *Eat This Book* (Grand Rapids: Eerdmans, 2006), 10–11.
8. Romans 12:2

Chapter 2: "A Thousand Steps" Between Us and God

1. Max Lucado, *God's Promises for You* (Nashville: Thomas Nelson, 2006), 171.
2. See Deuteronomy 30:14.
3. I once heard the late Rich Mullins describe Jesus this way. I'm blessed to know a handful of gutsy Christ-followers who share this distinction.
4. Frank C. Laubach, *Letters by a Modern Mystic* (Grand Rapids: Revell, 1958), 47–48.
5. Howard Baker, *Soul Keeping* (Colorado Springs: NavPress, 1998), 59.

6. A.W. Tozer, *The Pursuit of God* (Camp Hill, PA: Christian Publications, Inc., 1982), 16.

7. C. S. Lewis, *The Weight of Glory* (New York: HarperOne, 1942); see paragraph 13, 16–17.

8. See "20 Famous Quotes by John Wesley," © 2011 at www.worldofquotes.com.

9. John Wesley, "Sermon 78: Spiritual Idolatry." *The Sermons of John Wesley: 1872 Edition*, paragraph 6 (see at http://wesley.nnu.edu/john-wesley/the-sermons-of-john-wesley-1872-edition, Wesley Center for Applied Theology, Northwest Nazarene University; Nampa, ID,1999).

10. John Wesley, "Journal," 24 May 1738, in *A Diary of Readings,* ed. John Baillie (New York: Collier, 1955), 73.

11. Kenneth J. Collins, *A Real Christian: The Life of John Wesley* (Nashville: Abingdon, 1999), 51.

12. "John Wesley: Methodical Priest" (08/08/2008 at www.christianitytoday.com).

13. John Wesley, "Journal," 24 May 1738, in *A Diary of Readings,* ed. John Baillie (New York: Collier, 1955), 73.

14. See Deuteronomy 30:14.

15. See Howard Baker, *Soul Keeping* (Colorado Springs: NavPress, 1998), 22–24.

Chapter 3: The Bestseller Many Won't Read

1. e.g., 1 Timothy 2:11–12; 1 Corinthians 6:9–10; Colossians 3:22; Matthew 10:34–38

2. We'll go into this in depth in Part Two.

3. Family Safe Media, adapted from "Pornography Statistics." www.familysafemedia.com/pornography_statistics.html.

4. Ibid.

5. The Barna Research Group, Ltd., "New Marriage and Divorce Rates Released," © 2009, www.barna.org/barna-update/article/15-familykids/42-new-marriage-and-divorce-statistics-released.

6. The Pew Forum on Religion and Public Life, "Report 1: Religious Affiliation," © 2010, http://religions.pewforum.org/reports.

7. Ibid.

8. Ibid.

9. On the *Leno* story, see Clayton Hardiman, "Bible Literacy Slipping, Experts Say," http://home.snu.edu/~hculbert/literacy.htm (Southern Nazarene University, Bethany, OK, © 2009; accessed 10/05/2009). See also "Matthew, Mark, Luke and Ringo," http://2timothy1-6.blogspot.com/2011/10/matthew-mark-luke-and-ringo.html. (Spoken Word Ministries, © 2011; accessed 10/11/2011).

10. *The O'Reilly Factor*, "Personal Story Segment: More with Bill Maher" (09/30/2010, © 2010, Fox News Network).

11. See Genesis 6–9.

12. See Exodus 14.

13. See Jonah 1–4.

14. From SBC VOICES, blog post by SELAHV (10/01/10).

15. David Kinnaman and Gabe Lyons, *unChristian: What a New Generation Really Thinks About Christianity . . . and Why It Matters* (Grand Rapids: Baker, 2007), 18.

16. Marcus J. Borg, *The Heart of Christianity* (San Francisco: HarperSanFrancisco, 2003), 6.13.

17. Dr. Henrietta C. Mears, *What the Bible Is All About* (Ventura, CA: Regal, 1998), 11–12.

18. Marcus J. Borg, *Reading the Bible for the First Time* (New York: HarperOne, 2001), 22–23.

19. Joshua Harris, *Dug Down Deep* (Colorado Springs: Multnomah, 2010), 63–64.

20. Kay Arthur, *How to Study Your Bible* (Eugene, OR: Harvest House, 1994), 9, 15.

21. Scot McKnight, *The Blue Parakeet: Rethinking How You Read the Bible* (Grand Rapids: Zondervan, 2008), 87.

22. Mears, *What the Bible Is All About*, 23.

23. Donald Miller, "Why the Bible Is a Tough Book for Americans" (www.donmilleris.com, 8/26/10).

24. Brian D. McLaren, *A Generous Orthodoxy* (Grand Rapids: Zondervan, 2004), 177–178.

25. U.S. Bureau of Labor Statistics, Web Report (www.bls.gov, 02/23/10).

26. This is how Pastor Sean Dunn describes his encounters with God's Word at the beginning of his book *I Want the Cross!* (Grand Rapids: Revell, 2001), 2. It's what I experience too.

Chapter 4: From Temptation to Turmoil

1. Henry T. Blackaby and Richard Blackaby, *Experiencing God Day-By-Day* (Nashville: B&H, 1997), 328.

2. Gerald G. May, MD, *Addiction and Grace* (San Francisco: HarperCollins, 1988), 3–4.

3. Ibid.

4. See Romans 7.

5. e.g., see Mark 2:17.

6. Romans 3:10–18 *The Message*

7. Luke 12:2–3

8. 1 Corinthians 10:13

9. David Wilkerson, *Victory Over Sin and Self* (Grand Rapids: Revell, 1994), 25.

10. Our findings about men are dead-on with a survey conducted by the Catholic Church. They differ on the struggle women face most; according to the Vatican, pride is number one for women. (*BBC News*, "Two Sexes 'Sin in Different Ways,'" reported 02/18/09).

11. The question was specific to the temptation(s) they'd faced the previous day; response choices were yes, no, and some yes/some no.

12. The exact question was "Is thinking about temptation as bad as committing it?"

13. That is, we see in the data the correlations between higher Bible engagement and more awareness of temptation—as defined as higher reported number of temptations and minutes being tempted.

14. Number of temptations and minutes feeling tempted.

15. Mean average: 12.2

16. Mean average: 11.9

17. Mean average: 10.4

18. This is the temptation that had the most impact on their lives. Essentially, we were asking, "How long was this temptation an issue for you—how long was it playing out in your spiritual life?"

19. We noted that only twelve respondents listed temptation as a known hindrance to Bible engagement. Certainly they acknowledge temptation as a factor of (general) struggle—what they hadn't been noticing was its effect on when and how they engaged God's Word.

20. Galatians 5:16–18 NIV 1984

21. 2 Corinthians 5:17

22. 2 Corinthians 7:1

23. Dr. Larry Crabb, *66 Love Letters: A Conversation with God That Invites You into His Story* (Nashville: Thomas Nelson, 2009), 254–255.

Chapter 5: Breakthroughs for the Broken

1. J. I. Packer, *Rediscovering Holiness* (Ann Arbor, MI: Servant, 1992), 89.

2. 1 John 3:2

3. InterVarsity Staff, *Grow Your Christian Life* (Downers Grove, IL: IVP Connect, 1962), 83.

4. Romans 7:15, 18–20

5. 2 Corinthians 12:7–9 *The Message*

6. David Barshinger, a PhD candidate at Trinity Evangelical Divinity School, provided research and insights on the life of Paul. Portions adapted from David Barshinger, "Frustrated—Again!" in *Breakaway* (August 2005): 8–10.

7. See Philippians 3:12.

8. See Romans 5:12–13.

9. Philippians 3:13–14

10. 2 Corinthians 12:9

11. Romans 6:13–14 NIV 1984

12. See Ephesians 4:22–32.

13. Erwin W. Lutzer, *Your Eternal Reward* (Chicago: Moody, 1998), 58.

14. J. I. Packer, *Rediscovering Holiness* (Ann Arbor, MI: Servant, 1992), 90.

15. 1 Chronicles 21:1

16. Zechariah 3:1

17. 1 John 3:8

18. John 8:44

19. Charles F. Stanley, *When the Enemy Strikes* (Nashville: Thomas Nelson, 2004), 6.

20. Ibid.

21. See chapter 4.

22. I'm convinced Gene fell prey to what Arnie calls "Satan's veil." (Take a look at 2 Corinthians 3:12–18 for a snapshot of what he's talking about.)
23. Job 1:12
24. Hebrews 2:14
25. A. Scott Moreau, *Essentials of Spiritual Warfare* (Colorado Springs: Shaw, 2000), 111.
26. C. S. Lewis, *Mere Christianity* (San Francisco: HarperSanFrancisco, 1952, via C. S. Lewis Pte. Ltd), 32.
27. For instance, see Philippians 2:12–13.
28. "Kelly" and "Jeff" are pseudonyms. Their names were changed to protect their identities. Margie Younce, a writer and a program director for a nonprofit social services outreach in West Virginia, contributed to this story.
29. Mark 12:30
30. Romans 12:11–13 *The Message*

Chapter 6: Radically Relational (Not Too Religious)

1. See Les Sussman, *Praise Him! Christian Music Stars Share Their Favorite Verses From Scripture* (New York: St. Martin's Press, 1998), 155–164.
2. Ruth Haley Barton, *Sacred Rhythms: Arranging Our Lives for Spiritual Transformation* (Downers Grove, IL: InterVarsity, 2006), 49.
3. James 1:17 NKJV
4. See Matthew 22:37.
5. Doug Banister, *Sacred Quest* (Grand Rapids: Zondervan, 2001), 14–15.
6. John 17:21
7. Genesis 1:26
8. Banister, ibid.
9. Genesis 2:18
10. See Matthew 22:37–40.
11. Dr. Henry Cloud, *Changes That Heal* (Grand Rapids: Zondervan, 1992), 49.
12. 2 Corinthians 5:17
13. Matthew 7:21–23
14. See Matthew 7:15.
15. This is also confirmed by both the Barna Research Group and the Gallup poll.
16. Regarding the way we relate to others, Paul says: "If someone is caught in a sin, you who live by the Spirit should restore that person gently" (Galatians 6:1). In other words, we must strive to nudge, not judge, one another.
17. Matthew 7:16–17, 20

Chapter 7: Finding the Real God of Scripture

1. Paraphrased from Dietrich Bonhoeffer, *Life Together* (New York: Harper & Row, 1954), 83.
2. Ian Morgan Cron, *Chasing Francis: A Pilgrim's Tale* (Colorado Springs: NavPress, 2006), 30.
3. Ibid., 31.

4. Ibid., 55.
5. Revelation 3:16
6. Cron, ibid., 191.
7. Matthew 28:18–20 *The Message*

Chapter 8: Vertical Conversations

1. Eugene H. Peterson, *The Message* (Colorado Springs: NavPress, 2002), 11.
2. Dr. Henrietta C. Mears, *What the Bible Is All About* (Ventura, CA: Regal, 1998), 21.
3. Daniel 11:32 NKIV
4. See John 8:44; Revelation 12:10.
5. Psalm 33:4
6. Quoted in Mears, *What the Bible Is All About*, 9.
7. *Webster's New World Dictionary of the American Language, Second College Edition* (New York: William Collins and World Publishing Co., 1978).
8. Eugene H. Peterson, *Eat This Book* (Grand Rapids: Eerdmans, 2006), 10–11.
9. Henry T. Blackaby, *Experiencing God Day-by-Day* (Nashville: B&H, 1998), 110.
10. Ruth Haley Barton, *Sacred Rhythms: Arranging Our Lives for Spiritual Transformation* (Downers Grove, IL: InterVarsity, 2006), 50.
11. Romans 12:2
12. See Daniel 7:28.
13. See Luke 2:19, 51.
14. C. S. Lewis, *Mere Christianity* (San Francisco: HarperSanFrancisco, 1952, via C.S. Lewis Pte. Ltd), 164.
15. 1 Corinthians 13:12–13 *The Message*
16. Dr. Mary Spaulding, interview with Michael Ross (05/21/11).
17. See Matthew 7:13–14 *The Message*.
18. Woodrow Kroll, *How to Find God in the Bible Companion Study* (Lincoln, NE: Back to the Bible, 2006), 55.

Chapter 9: Giant Squid and Bible Truth

1. Dr. Henrietta C. Mears, *What the Bible Is All About* (Ventura, CA: Regal, 1998), 24.
2. Matthew 6:22–23 *The Message*
3. See John 9.
4. Matthew 11:15
5. Kinnaman and Lyons, *unChristian,*18.
6. George Barna, "Six Megathemes Emerge from Barna Group Research in 2010," www.barna.org.
7. Kinnaman and Lyons, *unChristian*, 18–19, 24.
8. Frank C. Laubach, *Letters by a Modern Mystic* (Grand Rapids: Revell, 1958), 47–48.
9. Psalm 32:8
10. Proverbs 4:20–22

11. John 1:14

12. J. I. Packer, *God Has Spoken: Revelation and the Bible* (Downers Grove, IL: InterVarsity, 1979), 50–52.

13. Luke 21:33

14. Hebrews 4:12–13

15. 2 Peter 1:19–21

16. Mears, *What the Bible Is All About*, 23.

17. Psalm 33:6

18. John 1:1–5

19. 1 Peter 1:23–25

20. Richard C. Halverson, *No Greater Power* (Sisters, OR: Multnomah, 1986), 186.

21. John 14:6

22. Romans 10:17

23. 2 Timothy 3:14–17

24. Robert S. McGee, *The Search for Significance* (Houston: Rapha, 1990), 263–264.

25. Max Lucado, *God's Promises for You* (Nashville: Thomas Nelson, 2006), 51.

26. Quoted in Mears, *What the Bible Is All About*, 10.

27. Jeremiah 15:16

Chapter 10: Moving Beyond "ME"

1. W. Phillip Keller, *Sky Edge: Mountaintop Meditations* (Grand Rapids: Kregel, 1992), 177.

2. 2 Timothy 3:1–5 *The Message*

3. Todd Huston, interview by Michael Ross, March 1996. Portions adapted from Todd Huston, "More Than Mountains" in *Breakaway* (August 1996): 6–9.

4. 1 Peter 3:8

5. Matthew 22:37–40

6. John 21:15

7. 1 John 4:9–10

8. See chapter 6.

9. Philippians 4:19

Chapter 11: Regaining the Wonder

1. Eugene O'Neill, *The Great God Brown* (Grand Rapids: Chosen, 2010), 58.

2. Matthew 25:35–36

3. Matthew 16:24–26

4. Hebrews 1:3

5. Romans 12:1–2 *The Message*

6. Matthew 6:9–13

7. See chapter 8.

8. See Genesis 2:21.

9. E.g., see Genesis 3:8.

10. Max Lucado, *The Great House of God* (Nashville: Word, 1997), 186.

11. Matthew 6:9
12. Genesis 48:15; 22:8; Judges 6:24; Exodus 15:26; 17:8–16
13. Revelation 1:8; Isaiah 7:14; 9:6; 1 Samuel 2:2; 1 John 3:14
14. Hebrews 11:3; Exodus 3:14; Isaiah 45:5
15. See J. I. Packer, *Knowing God* (Downers Grove, IL: InterVarsity, 1973), 15–16.
16. Hebrews 1:3
17. John 14:9, paraphrased
18. Luke 18:13
19. O'Neill, *The Great God Brown,* 58.
20. See Ephesians 4:22–32.
21. Proverbs 16:3
22. See Romans 12:2.
23. Isaiah 9:6 KJV

Chapter 12: Managing the "Dark Side"

1. David Wilkerson, *Victory Over Sin and Self* (Grand Rapids: Revell, 1994), 9.
2. Judges 2:11
3. Judges 2:16
4. Romans 3:23
5. Flip back to our discussions in chapters 4 and 5 for reminders.
6. See Philippians 3:13.
7. See Hebrews 12:1.
8. Jeremiah 31:34
9. See Philippians 3:7–8 NKJV.
10. Charles Haddon Spurgeon, quoted in Calvin Miller, *The Book of Jesus* (New York: Simon & Schuster, 1996), 51–52.
11. Ibid.
12. See Romans 7:13–8:1.

Chapter 13: Getting Unstuck Again . . . and *Again*

1. Matthew 18:12–14 *The Message*
2. Matthew 4:3 *The Message*
3. Matthew 4:4
4. See Walter Wangerin Jr., *The Book of God* (Grand Rapids: Zondervan, 1996), 623.
5. Matthew 4:6 *The Message*
6. Ted Miller, *The Story* (Carol Stream, IL: Tyndale, 1986), 316.
7. See Matthew 4:7.
8. Matthew 4:9 *The Message*
9. See Matthew 4:10.
10. From Deuteronomy 6:13
11. Story adapted from its telling in Michael Ross, *Tribe: A Warrior's Heart* (Carol Stream, IL: Tyndale, 2004), 89–90.
12. Ephesians 6:17

13. Manfred Koehler, pastor and former missionary to Mexico, provided research, writing, and insights in this section, based on Ephesians 6:10–18. Portions adapted from Michael Ross and Manfred Koehler, "Suiting Up for Battle" in *Breakaway* (March 2006):18–21.

14. See Psalm 84:11.

15. See Galatians 2:20.

16. See Hebrews 4:12.

17. See John 14:6.

18. See 2 Corinthians 5:21.

19. Matthew 11:28–30

20. See Romans 5:12–14.

21. See John 10:10.

22. We referenced this veil in describing Satan's designs and tactics in chapter 5.

23. James 1:13–15

24. David Wilkerson, *Victory Over Sin and Self* (Grand Rapids: Revell, 1994), 23.

25. Romans 6:12–14

26. Patrick A. Means, *Men's Secret Wars* (Grand Rapids: Revell, 1999), 176.

27. 1 John 1:9

28. Means, *Men's Secret Wars,* 177–178.

29. Ibid., 225–226.

30. Robert S. McGee, *The Search for Significance,* Student Edition (Nashville: W, 2003), 105.

31. Max Lucado, *He Still Moves Stones* (Dallas: Word, 1993), 110.

Chapter 14: Throwing Out the Formulas

1. Matthew 7:13–14 *The Message*

2. My Nebraska friend Johanna Pankonin shared this story with me.

3. Bob Briner, *Roaring Lambs* (Grand Rapids: Zondervan, 1993), 29–30.

4. Philip Yancey, *Reaching for the Invisible God* (Grand Rapids: Zondervan, 2000), 109–110.

5. Ibid.

6. See Titus 3:5.

7. 1 Corinthians 12:12

8. Matthew 10:30–31

9. John 10:14–15

10. See Isaiah 62:4.

11. Mark 12:30

12. Hebrews 12:1

13. 1 Corinthians 16:13

14. 1 Corinthians 13:11

15. 1 John 5:3–5

Arnie Cole (EdD, Pepperdine) is the CEO of Back to the Bible and director of research and development for the Center for Bible Engagement. He has spent much of his professional life tracking trends of human behavior and developing programs that can help change negative behaviors. He and his wife, Char, are the parents of adult children and operate Still Waters Ranch, an equestrian center that serves as a community outreach. The Coles live near Lincoln, Nebraska.

Michael Ross is an award-winning journalist and bestselling author. He writes, edits, and manages Back to the Bible's book publishing efforts and is a former editor of *Breakaway* magazine, published by Focus on the Family. He has authored and collaborated on more than 30 books, including *What Your Son Isn't Telling You*. Michael and his family live in Lincoln, Nebraska. Visit his website: www.michaelrossbooks.com.

DAILY
SPIRITUAL
GROWTH
JUST THE WAY
you NEED IT!

Get Unstuck Today.

Another Valuable Resource to Help Men Become *Unstuck*

A Rallying Call for Men to Ignite a Life of Strength and Honor

"Men today are discouraged, exhausted, and question their worth," says successful entrepreneur and ministr leader Vance Brown. Instead of letting these men fall by the wayside, Brown passionately sounds a call, a battle cry for men to join his Band of Brothers—men who follow Christ no matter the cost. Here is a battle plan for men who are ready to do something extraord nary with their lives and heed God's call. An excellent resource for men's small groups as well as individual use.

No Matter the Cost by Vance Brown with John Blase